Locke: An Introduction

LOCKE
An Introduction

John W. Yolton

Basil Blackwell

© John W. Yolton, 1985

First published 1985

Basil Blackwell Ltd
108 Cowley Road, Oxford OX4 1JF, UK

Basil Blackwell Inc.
432 Park Avenue South, Suite 1505,
New York, NY 10016, USA

British Library Cataloguing in Publication Data
Yolton, John W.
  1. Locke, John, 1632–1704
  I. Title
  192   B1297

Library of Congress Cataloging in Publication Data
Yolton, John W.
  John Locke, an introduction.
  Bibliography: p.
  Includes index.
  1. Locke, John, 1632–1704. I. Title.
B1297.Y59   1985   192   84–24620

ISBN 0–631–13376–3
ISBN 0–631–14062–X (pbk.)

Typeset by Oxford Publishing Services, Oxford
Printed in Great Britain by Page Bros., Norwich

For Jean

Contents

Preface   ix
Abbreviations   xi
Introduction   1
   The Red Trunk   6
   Philoclea and Philander   8
   Locke's Portrait   10
1 Moral Man and Forensic Person   17
   Natural Traits of Mind   19
   The Affective Part of the Mind   21
   Does the Man or the Soul Think   24
   The Person   28
2 Moral Rules and Standards   34
   Moral Education   34
   Reason and Moral Truths   39
   Reason as Natural Revelation   45
3 The Individual Socialized   51
   Action Words as Social Archetypes   53
   Social Groupings   56
   The Humanity of the Law of Nature   59
   The Power of the Community   64
   Private Property and Public Power   67
   Conclusion   71
4 The Rationality of Religion   74
   Civil and Religious Authority   74
   Articles of Faith and Scriptural Virtue 78
   Faith and Reason   82
   The Problem of the Criterion   87
5 The Metaphysics of Locke's Thought   92

   Metaphysics and Theology 93
   Secular Metaphysics: Tradition Modified 98
   Causes as Powers 111
   Conclusion 115
6 The Science of Mind 117
   Locke's Method: Its Relation to Science and Logic 119
   The Development of Awareness 124
   The Active Mind 131
7 Ideas and Knowledge 140
   Experience and the Reality of Knowledge 140
   What are Locke's Ideas? 148
   Conclusion 151
Bibliography: Locke's Major Works 154
Further Reading 155
Index 157

Preface

This study of the thought of John Locke is written with the student and general reader in mind. I have tried to be as non-technical as possible in my discussions of his writings, and I have tried to follow Locke's advice on how to read a text, attempting a sympathetic understanding of what he says. Criticism of his doctrines has not been my goal, although in places I do try to show some of the difficulties with what he says or fails to say. Some readers may feel I am not critical enough, especially with some of those doctrines that have been the focus of so much attention by centuries of philosophers. In presenting these doctrines, I have eschewed reference to and discussion of many of the stereotyped labels assigned to Locke by historians of philosophy. What is needed, I think, is an understanding of what Locke says, unencumbered by traditional interpretations. If this study is successful, each reader will be able, after working through my account, to go back to Locke's texts and evaluate my interpretations and those of other commentators.

The range of Locke's writing and interests, like the range of his activities, is so broad, the subjects he treats are so diverse, that a reader who is interested in just one aspect of his thought tends to lose sight of the location of that aspect in the total body of his writing. Thus, I have tried to cover a wide span of his writing, starting from his views on morality and the distinction between man and person (on which so much of his moral and political views are based). I have then worked through his views on education, especially moral education, and shown how those views fit into his social and political writings. His writings on religion, especially the long controversy with the Bishop of

Worcester, are presented, together with some of the metaphysical concepts Locke accepted and rejected. A chapter on the science of mind looks at his cognitive psychology. The study ends with a brief examination of the role and nature of ideas in his account of knowledge.

A brief bibliography of further reading is given, but the best works to consult are the works of Locke, which are also listed in the bibliography.

My special thanks go, as always, to my wife, to whom this study is dedicated.

Abbreviations

The following short titles have been used for citing from the writings of Locke. Unless otherwise indicated, quotations are from the 1823 edition of *The Works of John Locke* (10 vols). For full titles of works cited, and details of editions used, see the Bibliography.

Discourse	"A Discourse on Miracles", first published in *Posthumous Works*, 1706.
Education	*Some Thoughts concerning Education*, 1693. Axtell's edition.
Essay, followed by number of book, chapter, and section; e.g., 2.4.17.	*Essay concerning Human Understanding*, 1690. Nidditch's edition.
Letter	*A Letter concerning Toleration*, 1689.
Reasonableness	*The Reasonableness of Christianity*, 1695.
Letter to the Bishop	*Letter to Edward Lord Bishop of Worcester*, 1697.
Reply	*Mr. Locke's Reply to the Right Reverend the Bishop of Worcester's Answer to His Letter*, 1697.

Second Reply	*Mr. Locke's Reply to the Right Reverend the Bishop of Worcester's Answer to His Second Letter*, 1699.
Two Treatises, Second Treatise, or TI and TII, followed by a chapter number, as TI:34 or TII:9.	*Two Treatises of Government*, 1690. Laslett's edition.
Two Tracts	*John Locke: Two Tracts on Government*, edited by Philip Abrams, 1967.

Introduction

In an insightful essay on how to read a text, Locke warns against interpreting an author's words "by the notions of our philosophy". To read the texts of other authors in that way "is not the way to find their sense, in what they delivered, but our own, and to take up, from their writings, not what they left there for us, but what we bring along with us in ourselves".[1] Locke was writing about St Paul's Epistles, but his warnings and recommendations for understanding those writings is sound advice to follow in reading Locke himself. To understand an author requires us to "understand his terms, in the sense he uses them, and not as they are appropriated, by each man's particular philosophy, to conceptions that never entered the mind" of that author (*ibid.*). From the author's own words we should "paint his very ideas and thoughts in our minds".

To acquire such an understanding of an author, we should be on the alert for words in that text which have special meanings, doctrines whose signification differs from other similar ones then or now. It is also helpful to uncover, if we can, information about the "occasion of his writing" and the "temper and circumstances" of the people for whom he wrote (*ibid.*, p. 4). In addition, some sense of the author himself, his experiences, his attitudes and values, may be useful.

Locke scholarship since the 1950s has filled in much of the context for Locke's published books. His notebooks, the catalogue of his library, and his extensive correspondence have enabled us to reconstruct his reading, his composition, and his early thinking on various topics which later took form in his books. The account of his thought and doctrines given in the following chapters is written against the background of the discoveries and reconstructions of this recent scholarship. In this introduction, I want to raise the question, "what sort of man was Locke?" Only a full-scale historical and psychological biography can answer that question adequately, but the lines of an answer can be suggested by noting certain aspects of his personality as revealed by his reactions to his reading and to his critics, by the epitaph he composed for his gravestone, and by several vignettes taken from his correspondence.

Much of the writing and publishing of the seventeenth century was polemical, tracts and pamphlets written quickly as responses to a current controversy. Publication was rapid, a tract and its reply frequently appearing in quick succession. Exchanges might continue through several more tracts, all within one year or at most two. Locke's writing was often of this kind, begun as a response to some publication, even if the final version went well beyond the particular controversy which first started him thinking. Thus, when Edward Bagshaw published his *The Great Question concerning Things Indifferent in Religious Worship* (1660), Locke wrote two responses, one a point-by-point refutation of Bagshaw, the other a more theoretical offshoot of the detailed reaction. These tracts were never published by Locke (they have only recently been edited and published),[2] but they are an early example of Locke's polemical style of writing and of the way in which his reactions to his reading led him to formulate views of his own on issues and doctrines. Lectures he gave as Moral Censor at the University of Oxford in the early 1660s probably reflected some of his earlier thoughts, and enabled him to extend and modify them – those on moral laws, the law of nature and our knowledge of God.[3] His well-known treatise on politics, *Two Treatises of Government* (1690), either began as a reaction to Robert Filmer's *Patriarcha, or The Natural Power of Kings* (1680) or (the more exciting possibility suggested by Peter Laslett and slowly gaining acceptance) as a direct reaction to political events in England.[4] Locke's *Some Thoughts concerning Education* (1693) arose out of and consisted in large part of letters he wrote at the request of his close friend Edward Clarke for advice on how to raise and educate ("govern" was the term used then) his son. The tracts on money were very much topical responses to an economic crisis.[5] The *Essay concerning Human Understanding* (1690) began as a response to certain questions which emerged from a small discussion group to which Locke belonged.

The posthumous *Examination of P. Malebranche's Opinion*,[6] reflects Locke's concern with the nature of ideas (an important technical term in the account of knowledge), his response to the running debate between Malebranche and Antoine Arnauld[7] (a debate Locke was following closely as he put the *Essay* into final shape), and to Malebranche's British follower, John Norris. Two drafts of a direct response to Norris were among Locke's papers.[8] Locke marked up his copy of Sergeant's *Solid Philosophy Asserted*[9] (a heavy critique of Locke's philosophy in general), filling the margins with a variety of comments and criticisms. The third set of Thomas Burnet's *Remarks* on Locke's *Essay* also stimulated him to pen marginal responses in his copy of that work.[10] The only published responses of any length to his critics were Locke's replies to Bishop Stillingfleet's attack.[11]

These various unpublished and published responses to his critics range through heavy sarcasm and satire to polite but firm rejection. There are a few brief comments by Locke in two of his publications, general, dismissive remarks, suggesting that he did not find much of value in what his critics said. A brief, peevish note to Burnet's first set of *Remarks* was added at the end of Locke's second response to Stillingfleet, *Mr. Locke's Reply to the Right Reverend the Lord Bishop of Worcester's Answer to His Letter*. That note ended with this comment:

> If any one finds any thing in my Essay to be corrected, he may, when he pleases, write against it; and when I think fit I will answer him. For I do not intend my time shall be wasted at the pleasure of every one, who may have a mind to pick holes in my book, and show his skill in the art of confutation.[12]

The "Epistle to the Reader" of his *Essay* had earlier signalled Locke's attitude toward his critics.

> But what forwardness soever I have to resign any Opinion I have, or to recede from any thing I have Writ, upon the first evidence of any error in it; yet this I must own, that I have not had the good luck to receive any light from those Exceptions, I have met with in

print against any part of my Book, nor have, from any thing has been urg'd against it, found reason to alter my Sense in any of the Points [that] have been question'd.[13]

The extended replies to Stillingfleet, and the seriousness with which Locke took those charges (though his comments do contain wit and sarcasm too) may have been due to his worries about the claims made by Stillingfleet that his doctrines were a threat to religion. Locke's doctrines were criticized for the same reason by other writers; those doctrines (but not, I think, the man) were seen as a danger to orthodox beliefs. Reactions to most of his doctrines in the *Essay* filled the presses from early in 1690 to the end of that century, and many of his doctrines and his vocabulary are traceable well into the eighteenth century. Locke's doctrines were called most of the bad names of the day: sceptical, Socinian, deist, Hobbist, even atheistical. His *Reasonableness of Christianity* was banned by the Grand Jury of Middlesex in 1697, and the *Essay* was censored by some of the Heads of Colleges at Oxford in 1703.[14] As late as 1768, the *Essay* was placed on the *Index of Prohibited Books* by the Royal Censor Board in Portugal.[15]

Locke's books did receive praise and even public defence. Several books were dedicated to him soon after publication of the *Essay*, such as LeClerc's *Ontologia* (1692) and Burthogge's *Essay upon Reason* (1694). William Molyneux had warm praise for Locke and the *Essay* in the dedication to his work on optics, *Dioptrica Nova* (1692). Letters to Locke contain other praise, as well as suggestions (especially from Molyneux) for additions and changes to the *Essay*. Correspondents in France and Holland spread his reputation, as did the translators of many of his books into French and Latin. Reviews in the French-language journals also helped in the dissemination of his thought, provoking other critical reactions.

The temptation is to think of Locke as a man who suffered criticism poorly, who, despite his oft-proclaimed love of truth, only responded favourably to praise or to the comments of friends. There were some critics of his books who may be classified as "radical", "misguided", or even "malicious", but there were others who did raise and press important and valid questions. He profited little if at all from such writings. The peevish, sarcastic dismissals of Burnet, Sergeant and Norris, the general announcement in the *Essay* that he had seen nothing of value against that work, contrast strikingly with the expressions of modesty and love of truth he so often assumed.

The Epitaph he composed for himself spoke of being content with his modest lot and of being educated sufficiently to satisfy the demands solely of truth. The letter to Edward Clarke which was printed as a kind of preface to *Some Thoughts concerning Education* speaks of "the Meanness of these Papers, and my just Distrust of them", and confesses: "I should not be sorry, even for your sake, if some one abler and fitter for such a Task, would in a just Treatise of Education, suited to our English Gentry, rectifie the Mistakes I have made in this."[16] The "Epistle to the Reader" of the *Essay* characterizes that work as a kind of hawking, but for "Larks and Sparrows", not for "nobler Game". He professes in this same place to be "liable to mistakes", urging the reader to test this work for truth. He also disclaims anything new or instructive in that work, stressing that it was not written for "those that had already mastered this subject" (of the nature of the human understanding), nor for "men of large thoughts and quick apprehensions"; rather, the *Essay* was written "for my own Information, and the Satisfaction of a few Friends". What the *Essay* contains is "spun out of my own coarse thoughts", fitted "to Men of my own size". The most famous passage proclaiming these modest assessments of his work is his talk of the "master-builders" (Boyle, Sydenham, Huygens, Newton), in which he characterizes himself as *"an Under-Labourer in clearing Ground a little, and removing some of the Rubbish, that lies in the way to Knowledge"*.

Whether these various statements are genuine, whether they are more a formal, somewhat artificial literary device, they do stand in rather sharp contrast to his easy rejection of almost all criticism. At the same time, the essay style of writing, and even Locke's 'plain, historical method' of acquiring knowledge by observation and experimentation, *are* consistent with these claims. There may have been some insecurity on Locke's part about the areas he investigated, perhaps also about being an author. He did not publish anything until he was in his late 50s. Even then, *A Letter concerning Toleration, Some Thoughts concerning Education* and *Two Treatises of Government* were published anonymously, the latter only being acknowledged near the end of Locke's life. Some of the lateness of publication was due to his varied interests which pulled him between medicine, politics, science and philosophy. He also travelled extensively in France (once as a tutor to a young son of a friend), and he was for a number of years very busy in the household of Anthony Ashley Cooper, who became the Earl of Shaftesbury, fell from favour with the king, was suspected of a treasonable plot, and fled to Holland where he died.

Locke's close association with Shaftesbury naturally brought suspicion upon his head. The events that then unfolded around him are rather tense and exciting. He was expelled from his college, Christ Church, by order of the king himself. "Fled" may be too strong a word, but Locke did end up, by a route not entirely known, in Holland. It is at this point in the story that I want to introduce the first vignette of Locke, as a way of showing one facet of his personality.

THE RED TRUNK

Before leaving for Holland, Locke transferred some of his papers from his rooms in Christ Church to the house of his friend, James Tyrrell. Other papers were sent to Edward Clarke for disposal, for burning if Clarke thought it wise. He made a will and left for Clarke a short cipher to be used for referring to people secretly, in case that was ever needed. The urgency of his leaving England may have been increased, as Cranston suggests, by the arrest of Algernon Sidney, who was, among others, charged with writing "seditious and treasonable manuscripts".[17] Sidney had written against Filmer's *Patriarcha*; Locke may have already written, or sketched out, some of his *Two Treatises*, part of which was to be against Filmer. *Two Treatises* was also to defend the rights of the people against a ruler, under certain conditions. In a letter to Clarke of 26 August 1683, along with various instructions about papers, money, and his will, Locke referred to a sealed paper which Clarke would recognize by shape from what Locke had earlier told him.[18] "You may consider," Locke wrote, "whether you think it best to lie there or no." In a letter to Clarke from

Holland, dated 1 December 1683, Locke refers to "the chest that is now in Mrs. . . [probably Griggs] custody".[19] He had given the key to a friend, Dr Thomas. Locke says very mysteriously that "I either think or dreamt you enquired of me concerning the title of a treatise, part whereof is in Mr. Smith's hands, and it is *Tractatus de morbo Gallico*." The reference is clearly intentionally veiled. Locke says he has heard this work commended and that he would like to read it if there is a spare copy. The "Mr Smith" may be Locke himself. Peter Laslett has suggested that the title Locke used was a code name for part of *Two Treatises*.[20] Locke described this work in Clarke's letter as a work of 'physick'. "De Morbo Gallico" is also mentioned in two earlier letters to Dr Thomas, a fact that either lends credence to its being a work of medicine or is consistent with its being a cover name.[21] It is Dr Thomas who has the key to Locke's trunk, so either alternative could fit. But the veiled way Locke refers to this work in this letter to Clarke lends support to Laslett's suggestion, at least to the possibility that a work of Locke's is being cited.

Whether "De Morbo Gallico" is the same set of papers Locke wrote about in a later letter is not entirely clear, but the sense of urgency about some papers in a trunk increases. A mutilated letter of 1685 (when Locke was still in Holland) refers to "an hair portmanteau trunk" containing deeds and "the box you nailed up and sent thither". As well, Locke refers to "a very little red trunk of mine, not a foot I think nor eight inches long". Locke instructs Clarke to lock that box up in the hair trunk. He is concerned about box and trunk in still another letter to Clarke a month or so later. Then on 26 March/5 April 1685, there is a very worried, long, cryptic passage, clearly in coded language, about the red trunk. Clarke has apparently failed to follow Locke's instructions on what to do with the contents of that trunk (not all the correspondence between Locke and Clarke has survived). Pretending that the trunk contains drugs and chemical preparations, Locke says that "to speake freely to you, the same reason that makes him [Clarke] desire to keepe them makes me desire he should not."[22] The details of this long passage can be consulted in the *Correspondence*, but it is important to note that Locke even expresses fear for Clarke's children, should Clarke fail to follow Locke's instructions which were, apparently, either to destroy the papers or to get them out of Clarke's house. In a letter to Clarke of 23 April/3 May 1685, Locke says (referring to a letter from Clarke not preserved): "I am very glad my cosin Somers [i.e. Clarke], as you tell me, will punctually comply with my desires concerning the drugs and chimical preparations I write about."[23]

The full story of Locke's adventures in Holland (a story of disguises, of hiding, perhaps even of tricks, and frequent moves) makes fascinating reading. Besides giving some of the flavour of his political involvement, of his association with persons who challenged tradition, this incident of the red trunk and its mysterious contents suggests various features of Locke's person and personality. Cautious, meticulous, guarded, secretive, but also trusting and concerned for his close friend, Clarke, these same letters often contained thoughts on how to raise Clarke's son. Locke was also writing on toleration while in Holland, meeting regularly with a small discussion group, and completing his *Essay*. One other matter arises in a few of the early letters from Holland; references to Damaris Cudworth (later Lady Masham), with whom Locke had close emotional ties. Tracing a bit of that relationship, as it is revealed in their correspondence, reveals other facets of Locke's personality.

PHILOCLEA AND PHILANDER

There were a number of women who were attracted to Locke and for whom he obviously had strong affection. His letters to E.A. (probably Anne Evelegh) reveal Locke's emotions and interests.[24] These letters are rather formal, following some of the standard models for such letters, but Locke's feelings nevertheless seem genuine. There is also a fascinating draft letter to an unnamed woman which is a response to someone Locke had seen or observed but to whom he had not expressed his affection. This draft letter, addressed simply to 'Madam', begins:

> To catch the eys of forward gazers, or by degrees to fire a heart that courts its flames is the effect of an ordinary face, As what fire is there that cannot warme him that nearly approaches it, But M. to Captivate at a distance and takeing a heart (that supposd it self well fortified) without either surprise or seige is the priviledg only of your beauty which scorns to conquer ordinary ways . . .[25]

The letter continues in the same vein, highly charged with emotion. It was written in 1658 or 1659, when Locke was 26 or 27. The taking of Locke's heart was never again (so far as we know) so easily done.

Locke's most well-known relationship was with Damaris Cudworth, the daughter of the philosopher and theologian, Ralph Cudworth. Over 40 of her letters to Locke have survived, but we have very few of his to her. Whether we can infer anything from this absence of Locke's letters is hard to say, but it does mean that, except for some references Damaris makes in her letters, we cannot determine the contents of Locke's letters. Enough survives, however, to indicate that they had a close and strong attraction to each other.

Their letters range from discussion of various philosophical and religious books to the relative merits of reason or enthusiasm in faith, from classification of the mind–body relation in various authors to many ordinary events in their lives. Part of Locke's interest in Damaris was for her intellectual abilities. There is in Damaris's letters (all of which are signed 'Philoclea' and some of which speak of Locke as Philander or, in her verses, as Damon) a friendly, bantering tone. Sometimes she pretends to be angry with Locke. Locke, for his part, in one letter expressed concern at a fall she had taken, at other times he worries about the pains she frequently had in her head, sending her on one occasion some snuff which she had requested as a relief for those pains. There are often remarks in her letters (which begin in early 1682) to books of theology and philosophy, to treatises on the passions, to classical writers (e.g. Seneca) and to friendship. And when Locke indicates that he will be going to Tunbridge Wells (a well-known spa for taking the waters and for socializing), Damaris asks him to tell her who the beauties are there and who loves whom.

In a letter of 14 August 1682, Damaris refers to a question Locke had put in his last letter: "had she left her heart in London" when she visited Locke there? Her reply is "no", but not given in such a way as to discourage him. Locke had apparently sent her a book on navigation which she, not surprisingly, said she found of little interest. In other letters there are references to attempts they made to visit each other, to Locke's saying the thought of Damaris made him happy. In January 1683, Damaris sent Locke a long poem describing from her point of view the ups and downs of their relationship. There is also a verse reply by Locke. At about this time, the troubles of Shaftesbury and his death had taken place, and Locke went off (without telling Damaris how to write to him) to Holland. Absence did not help their relationship, although the correspondence does continue in a friendly way, with (as Damaris remarks) fewer letters from Locke. Her letters to him in Holland continue the pattern of remarks on books, on philosophical topics, on love and marriage. There were efforts made for her to come to Holland, but these proved unsuccessful. It is clear from some of her letters that their circle of friends in England knew and accepted the fact that Locke loved Damaris, but by June 1685 she writes as Lady Masham. How much of a surprise this was to Locke, we cannot say. She says that she had received his last letter while she was in the very church where she was soon to marry Sir Francis Masham, not perhaps the most tactful remark she could have made. She urges Locke to visit her and her new husband when Locke returns to England. By 15 September, Lady Masham remarks that Locke's letter responding to the announcement of her marriage differs remarkably in style from his previous letters! However, she still insists on preserving their friendship.

What the frustrations and indecisions may have been in the relationship with Locke which ended in such an abrupt decision on Damaris's part to marry a widower with eight children, we do not know. The fact that their friendship did survive her marriage (Locke eventually went to live with the Mashams at Sir Francis's home at Oates, living there from 1694 until his death in 1704), may tell us more about Damaris's views about love and marriage than it reveals of Locke's character. Nevertheless, this long-lasting friendship with Damaris must testify to the trust they had in each other, as well as to their many common interests.

LOCKE'S PORTRAIT

From Locke's correspondence we have been able to trace the mysterious and potentially dangerous episode of the red trunk. We have also sketched the relationship he had with Damaris Cudworth. The correspondence yields another episode in Locke's life worth noting, this time a curious, almost an amusing one. The question was, "who was the owner of Locke's portrait?"

In 1672, while painting a portrait of Shaftesbury, John Greenhill also painted Locke. When Locke went to France in 1675, he packed many of his possessions for storage, leaving them in various places. The portrait was left at Thanet House, Shaftesbury's London home. In a journal entry for 12 July 1679, Locke notes that he found at Thanet House all that he left there, "except my picture which he [Stringer, Shaftesbury's secretary] had removed to his house at Bexwells".[26] We hear again about this portrait in a letter Locke wrote from Holland on 28 February 1688 to Edward Clarke and his wife. Referring to Mr and Mrs Stringer as Thomas and Susan, Locke says he hears they are in London. He wonders why they have not written to him. About his *Essay*, then nearing completion, he says:

> When I print my book, as I think now I shall, I would have my picture before it; therefore, pray get the picture they [the Stringers] have of mine up to town whilst you are there, that I may take order to have a plate graved from it.[27]

Clarke wrote to Thomas Stringer, as requested, and received a very surprising reply. Stringer wrote a convoluted letter, refusing to give up the Greenhill picture. He offered a variety of reasons for keeping it: having it will force Locke to write letters to them, the portrait hangs among good company at Bexwells, and moreover, the title to the picture belongs to Stringer. There are other rationalizations for not acceding to Locke's request, including the suggestion that Locke's claim to want to use the portrait to make an engraving is just a "Colourable Excuse".[28]

Clarke sent Stringer's letter to Locke on 16 March. On 16 April, Locke wrote to Stringer. The Stringers had complained at not receiving any letters from Locke. To that, Locke says, with an eye upon his special situation in Holland:

> If I have forborne to write to any of my friends it has been purely out of regard to them, to whom I thought I could not doe either more civily, or more friendly then to leave it to them to judg, whether they thought it fit to hold any correspondence with me. . . .[29]

Locke also says that he kept up the correspondence with Mrs

Stringer "till she plainly said she would write noe more to me". Stringer is then chastised rather mildly about the portrait:

> If you beleive your self when you say I gave you my picture, I beseech you to consider, what you think of your self, when you deny it me upon this occasion; Sure I am you will never perswade any body else, that you think bona fide I gave it you whilst you dare not trust it again in my hands. For you will not finde any one who knows me, that will imagin, I deserve to be suspected of a designe to cheat any one of what is his, much lesse a friend of what I my self had given him.

Stringer's reply to this letter (30 April 1688) was a long, vituperative letter, out of all proportion to the tone of Locke's letter of 16 April. Locke characterizes this letter of Stringer as 'Civil and obleigeing'![30] It is as if Locke refuses to become angry. He asks to be remembered to Mrs Stringer and in other ways tries to be friendly. He does reply to many of Stringer's complaints. On the matter of the picture, Locke asks when and where and under what conditions he gave it to Stringer (while he denies that he did give it to him, the rest of the correspondence suggests that Locke may not have been so confident that he had not given it away). He enclosed this letter to Stringer in one he sent to Clarke on the same date. To Clarke, Locke comments:

> You will here enclosed find a letter to Mr. Stringer in answer to his about my picture. The truth is, he deals with me after a way I could scarce have believed under any other assurance but that of his own hand. He tells me his wife has it under my hand that I gave it to him. I am afraid he strains the matter too far, for having never purposed but to have that picture in my chamber in Oxford when I came to settle there I am sure I could never give it away in a letter to anyone, or say anything like it unless I were drunk when I writ it.[31]

But, Locke adds, "if you can, pray get a sight of that letter that I may know what it is for I have not the least remembrance of any the least thing towards it, nor can I believe it."

In a letter of 21 May to Clarke, Locke suggests that perhaps all that Mrs Stringer's claim that Locke had written a letter giving them the picture is based upon is the letter in which Locke asked to borrow the picture, thereby leading her to infer that Locke thought it did belong to the Stringers. Locke then details the whole account of his sitting for the picture, his intentions to have it at Christ Church, his denial that he ever gave it away, etc. As he had in one of the letters to Stringer, Locke offers as evidence of his title to the picture the fact that he paid 15 shillings for it.

On 19 June Clarke offered to intercede again and to try to get the matter resolved, assuring Locke that "I cannot find any thing Blameable in any of your Proceedings." In a still later letter (of 16 September), Clarke writes to Locke that he told the Stringers he thought there was no cause in anything Locke had written to call forth the angry response in Stringer's letter of 30 April. Clarke adds: "But I cannot gett a sight of That Letter of yours, which, conveys the unquestioned right you once had in the Picture." Why should both Locke and Clarke persist in their efforts to get a look at the letter the Stringers claimed they had, if Locke was so certain he had never given the title to that portrait away?

This somewhat bizarre incident was finally resolved, probably through the intervention of Mrs Clarke. Locke wrote to Mrs Stringer on 25 July 1689, trying to explain his annoyance about the picture and their claims, but then saying that he had recently seen the Greenhill portrait at a painter's shop. He assumed that it had been sent there so he could have the engraving made. Locke, rather strangely after the letters that have passed between them, wants Stringer's permission before he uses it for the engraving! Again we must ask why he should seek this permission if he thought he was all along in the right on his claim of ownership. Mrs Stringer responded on 29 July, saying the picture is at Locke's disposal. Clarke, too, wrote (on 30 July) assuring Locke that the Stringers did want Locke to use the picture, but Clarke says that Mr Stringer still claims the picture is his. A letter from Mrs Stringer on 9 August confirms that Mrs Clarke had convinced her to return the picture.

The extensive collection of letters between Locke and his many correspondents reveals other aspects of his life and character. After returning to England in 1688, he maintained letter contact with most of the friends he had made in Holland. He also corresponded with many people in France, and with friends and relatives in England. The subject matter of those letters ranged over details about the land he owned, investments of his money, medical advice and cures for ills, comments on recent publications in England and abroad, the state of the currency, trade and commerce, philosophical and religious questions. Those letters show an interest in and care for his friends, a respectful and helpful response to enquiries from strangers, and a persistent questioning and examination of serious intellectual topics. The picture we get from his letters is of a strong-willed man, a man of great curiosity, whose actions were frequently the occasion for self-analysis. We get a picture of an individual who was not passive at all, an active individual. Locke was not a frivolous man, nor does his correspondence reveal any aesthetic responses, though there is a strong interest in classical literature.

In saying, in his epitaph,[32] that reading his published writings will tell us whatever "there is to be said of him", Locke had in mind the thoughts, beliefs and principles contained there. It is time we turned to our study of those writings. We can do so now against the background of some of the features of Locke the man as revealed in his letters and in his comments about his critics and himself. The 'temper' of the man, some of his character traits, have emerged from this brief examination. We shall see how important for Locke's concept of the person were traits of character and natural inclinations. The person is at the centre of his philosophical, political, educational, moral and religious beliefs.

NOTES

1 See his introduction to his *Paraphrases of St. Paul's Epistles*, in *Works* (1823 edn) vol. VIII, p. 21.
2 *John Locke: Two Tracts on Government* (ed. Philip Abrams) (1967).
3 These early writings were not published until 1954, by W. von Leyden, as *Essays on the Law of Nature*.
4 See the Introduction to Peter Laslett's edition of *Two Treatises of Government* (1960).
5 He published three tracts on money in 1692 and in 1695. The title of the first of these tracts was *Some Considerations of the Consequences of the Lowering of Interest and Raising the Value of Money*. Patrick Kelly has edited these with introduction and notes for the *Clarendon Edition of The Works of John Locke* (in press).

6 In *Works* (1823 edn), vol. IX.
7 Malebranche published his *De la recherche de la Vérité* in 1678. Antoine Arnauld attacked that work in his *Des vrayes et des fausses idées* (1683). There then followed a number of replies and counter-replies.
8 For one of these, see Locke's *Remarks upon Some of Mr. Norris's Books*, published posthumously and now to be found in *Works* (1823), vol. X. The other, edited by Richard Acworth, is to be found in the *Locke Newsletter*, no. 2 (Summer 1971).
9 Locke's copy of Sergeant's book, with many marginal notes, is in the library of St John's College, Cambridge.
10 Thomas Burnet, *Third Remarks upon an Essay concerning Humane Understanding* (1699). Locke's copy of this work, with his marginal comments, is in the Yale University Library.
11 These can be found in *Works* (1823 edn), vol. IV.
12 *Ibid.*, p. 189.
13 See Peter H. Nidditch's edition of the *Essay* (1975), p. 11.
14 See my *John Locke and the Way of Ideas* (1956), pp. 11–13.
15 For a discussion of this, see "Locke's Suggestion of Thinking Matter and Some Eighteenth-Century Portuguese Reactions", by Jean S. and John W. Yolton *Journal of the History of Ideas* (1984).
16 *Some Thoughts concerning Education* (1693).
17 See Maurice Cranston, *John Locke, a Biography* (1957), pp. 227–9, for the details of Locke's move to and stay in Holland.
18 Letter 771, in *The Correspondence of John Locke*, ed. E.S. de Beer, vol. II (1976), p. 601.
19 Letter 773, *ibid.*, p. 606.
20 See Laslett's edition of *Two Treatises* (1960) pp. 45–66.
21 Letters 723 and 725, *Correspondence*, ed. de Beer, vol. II pp. 535,537.
22 Letter 817, *ibid.*, vol. II, p. 709.
23 Letter 822, *ibid.*, vol. II, p. 718. Cranston points out that Clarke was arrested on 8 June 1685, "charged with being in correspondence with traitors in Holland" (*Biography*, p. 253).
24 See *Correspondence*, ed. de Beer, vol. I, Letters 63,65,71,83,84,86.
25 Letter *ibid.*, vol. I, 45, p. 64–5.
26 Cranston, *Biography*, p. 187.
27 Letter 1020, *Correspondence* ed. de Beer, vol. III, p. 388.
28 Letter 1028, dated 12 March 1688, *ibid.*, p. 411.
29 Letter 1038, *ibid.*, p. 429.
30 Letter 1046, *ibid.*, p. 445.
31 Letter 1047, *ibid.*, p. 449.
32 The epitaph in Latin for his tombstone was first published in *The Works of John Locke* (3 vols., 1714). In translation it reads:

Stay, wayfarer, Near here lies John Locke. If you ask what sort of man he was, his answer is that he lived content with his modest lot. Educated in letters, he accomplished as much as satisfied the demands solely of truth. This you may learn from his writings; which will also tell you whatever else there is to be said of him, more truly than the doubtful praises of an epitaph. Any virtues he had were more slight than should encourage you, in praise of him, to follow his example; may his faults be interred with him. If a model of conduct you seek, you have it in the Gospels; if only of vices, look for it in no place: if of mortality (of what benefit it may be) assuredly you have it here and everywhere. That he was born in the year of Our Lord 1632 August 29th, died in the year of Our Lord 1704 October 28th, this tablet, that may itself soon perish, is a record.

1

Moral Man and Forensic Person

In a chapter of his *Essay concerning Human Understanding* devoted to a discussion of a traditional question, 'what is it that makes an individual or particular thing one thing?', Locke directs the topic onto the question of man. Remarking that a plant is *one* plant just because it has a particular organization of parts in one coherent body sharing in "one Common Life", he says that a plant continues to be and is recognised as being the same plant so long as it lives, so long as it "partakes of the same Life" (2.27.4). Even when the particles of the matter of that plant change and are replaced as the plant grows, the life of that plant marks the continuity and identity of, e.g., *that* particular dahlia.

Similarly with animals. While Locke dangerously (because it could sound like materialism) compared the animal body to a machine (e.g. a watch), the identity of both machine and animal lies in the "Organization, or Construction of Parts, to a certain end" (§5). The animal differs from the machine and is like a plant in having a common life throughout its existence. The fact that the parts, the biological parts, of the animal's body are always being added to and are growing does not affect the sameness, the oneness, of that animal, no more so than repairing, increasing, or changing the parts of a watch will alter its identity. What is important is the organization of parts, the purpose or end, and the movement or life of the whole organism.

In the same way, the sameness of a man consists in "Nothing but a participation of the same continued Life, by constantly fleeting Particles of Matter, in succession vitally united to the same organized Body" (§6). Just as plants and animals change and grow throughout a lifetime, so a man is in one life an embryo, an infant, a child, an adult, mad and sober, happy and sad. These different states and conditions happen to one individual, one biological creature, one man. The organized body and the organization of life are run by the physiology of the biological body, by the blood, nerves, muscles and other essential parts. The functioning of the live organism, even in man, was frequently referred to as the 'machine of the body'. Locke did not want to go into details of this physiology, but he says enough about it to indicate that he follows the accepted account, an account inherited from Descartes, Malebranche, and English anatomists such as Thomas Willis. That physiology was based on the concept of nerves as tubes with fluid flowing through them to and from the brain.

This account of the workings of the body is rather mechanical, but there was also a clear recognition of the close interaction between the physiology and the emotional and psychological states of man. The psychology was one of the faculties, specific cognitive processes for particular functions, e.g. sensation, memory, imagination, understanding. Along with these faculties there is for Locke a long list of mental operations, acts of the mind, e.g. considering, comparing, adding, abstracting, inferring, concluding. Some of the faculties were more closely tied to bodily functions than others. Locke raises the possibility that the workings of the physiology of the body may account for memory, for habits of thinking and acting, for our ability to act voluntarily, for different, felt experiences when we place a warm hand in cold water or a cold hand in warm water. The mechanism of the body can sometimes interfere with and be the cause of specific conscious experiences.

The body with the shape it has, is the most obvious and commonly used feature of what we call 'a man'. But we as men also have minds. 'Mind' is not a term Locke uses as synonymous with 'soul'. He tends to restrict 'soul' to the traditional notion of an immaterial substance. Such a substance for most orthodox religious believers then was the essential aspect of human beings. Locke did not think we had sufficient knowledge to say what such a substance was or what role it plays in our lives. Immaterial substance was a concept of metaphysics, not one open to experience, even to reflective experience. The body is clearly accessible to us, but so are our thoughts, beliefs, ideas, intuitions, intentions, doubts, reasonings, desires. Whereas the nerves, muscles, brain, heart and the activities of these component parts belong to our body, our thoughts, ideas, passions, etc., are ascribed to our mind. The mind is the source, often acting in tandem with the mechanism of the body, of these conscious items and the activities that help produce them, e.g. willing, believing, intending.

NATURAL TRAITS OF MIND

Within the domain of the mind, of consciousness, Locke finds differences. There is an area or a feature of the mind which is or can be under its control, but there is also an area which often works against and counter to our intentions. One feature of the mind which is part of its natural inheritance and which educators in particular must learn to work with is what Locke calls 'Tempers of Mind' (*Essay*, 2.20.3). In *Some Thoughts concerning Education*, he speaks of children's "original tempers" which education cannot wholly change: "God has stampt certain Characters upon Men's Minds, which, like their Shapes, may perhaps be a little mended; but can hardly be totally alter'd, and transform'd into the contrary" (§66). Children are born with a "Byass in their natural Temper" (§139), and the peculiarity of each mind distinguishes each from all others, just as much as does the face (§216). The educator must study children's natures and adjust the goal of education to what is possible in each case: "the business of Education" is "either to take off, or counter-balance" those natural traits. The general teaching techniques are invariant, but the specific method of teaching and guiding each child should be adapted to the child's natural temper: "there are possibly scarce two Children, who can be conducted by exactly the same method" (§216; cf.102).

In his 1677 essay, "Of Study", Locke stressed the same point: "There are peculiar endowments and natural fitnesses, as well as defects and weaknesses, almost in every man's mind."[1] It is important, Locke remarked in this same early essay, to learn how to "follow the bent and tendency of the mind itself" through a recognition of these "sympathies and antipathies" (*ibid.*, p. 414).

An understanding of the physiognomy of each mind will show us what general character traits and what course of life and employment we can hope to develop in each child. We should not try to make the "Gay Pensive and Grave, nor the Melancholy Sportive", the *Education* says (§66). Other unalterable frames of mind are listed in that work: stout, timorous, confident, modest, tractable, obstinate, curious, careless, quick and slow. Elsewhere this list is expanded by the following: fierce, mild, bold, bashful, compassionate, cruel, open and reserved. All these character traits have to be accepted and worked with in trying to guide the child to rationality, always the goal for Locke. Some acquired traits that the educator can encourage or eliminate are honesty, foolhardiness, courage, cowardice, censoriousness and contradictoriness. Whatever the precise lists are of character traits that are "stampt and unalterable" and of those that can be instilled by training, it should be clear that there is no inconsistency in Locke's view about what education can achieve. From the opening section of the *Education*, he talks of the "natural Genius" and temper all men have. He admits in that section that some few individuals have such a natural temper that almost unguided from the cradle they are "carried towards what is Excellent", but most individuals "are what they are, Good or Evil, useful or not, by their Education" (§1).

Locke makes the same point in *Of the Conduct of the Understanding*: "There is, it is visible, great variety in men's understandings, and their natural constitutions put so wide a difference between some men, in this respect, that art and industry would never be able to master".[2] The natural faculties we are born with lead us all to truth and right conduct. In this work, Locke also characterizes natural reason as the touchstone of truth. Wrong use and cultivation of this and our other faculties can lead astray even "some men of study and thought".[3] Because the proper training of our faculties is so fundamental to the subsequent course of our lives, education takes on great importance for Locke. We begin with different character traits but with equal natural faculties, which education can guide and develop. In this way, "the difference so observable in men's understandings and parts, does not arise so much from their natural faculties as acquired habits."[4]

THE AFFECTIVE PART OF THE MIND

Passions and desires are very much a part of human nature for
Locke, but a part in need of control and proper use. Just as the
state of our body, the physiological condition it is in and the
nature of its processes, can affect our awareness and mental state,
so can our passions, desires and inclinations. Locke's account of
man recognizes the control and direction which the affective side
of human nature can exert. There are affective forces as well as
physiological ones constituting a man. Both are natural parts of
our nature. There are "natural tendencies imprinted on the
Minds of Men", from the "very first instances of Sense and
Perception, there are some things, that are grateful, and others
unwelcome to them; some things that they incline to, and others
that they fly" (*Essay*, 1.3.3). We naturally seek that which is
pleasurable and shun that which is painful. Pleasure and pain
each encompasses a series. Pleasure includes satisfaction, delight,
happiness, while pain includes uneasiness, trouble, torment,
anguish and misery (2.7.2). Either can arise from the thoughts of
our mind or from whatever affects our bodies. It is God who has
arranged to have pleasure and pain in varying degrees accompany
all experiences, for in that way we can be "excited to" those
actions of thinking and moving in the world which also
characterize us (2.7.3). The pleasure-pain response serves as a
natural aid to our preservation and as a spur to action. Desire is
defined as "an *uneasiness* in the want of an absent good, in
reference to any pain felt, ease is that absent good" (2.21.31).
The "*uneasiness* of *desire*, fixed on some absent good"
determines our will and results in our acting (2.31.33).

There are different kinds of uneasinesses. Some are related to
the judgement we make and the strength of our desire for some
absent good, but others arise from "the pains of the Body from
want, disease, or outward injuries" (2.21.57). It is symptomatic
of Locke's attitude toward desires that he remarks about this
latter kind that they often "turn the course of Men's lives from
Virtue, Piety, and Religion, and what before they judge to lead to
happiness". Desire and passion can be put to work towards virtue
(at least some can), as Locke's *Education* urges, but in general

they are viewed as qualities of our nature which need careful watching. The *Essay* contrasts being content with things as they "minister to his Pleasures and Passions" with enquiry into the "Causes, Ends, and admirable Contrivances" of the world, as a way of acquiring the idea of God (1.4.22). He remarks that "sometimes a boisterous Passion hurries our Thoughts, as a Hurricane does our Bodies" (2.21.12). Love and anger and other violent passions are said to be able to run away with us (2.21.53). He also speaks of being under the power of an unruly passion. Passions are also said to interfere with the contemplation of truth and the pursuit of certainty. There are many passages where Locke recommends the suspension of the present satisfaction of a desire so that we can reach a sound judgement as to what we should do (2.21.53). Moderation and restraint of our passions is recommended.

In the *Education*, desires usually stand in opposition to reason. There, "the great Principle and Foundation of all Vertue and Worth, is placed in this. That a Man is able to *deny himself* his own Desires, cross his own Inclinations, and purely follow what Reason directs as best, tho' the Appetite lean the other way" (§33; cf.38). The difference between one man and another is not whether or not they have certain desires, but "the Power to govern, and deny ourselves" (§36). Learning to submit their desires to the parent's and tutor's reason is good and essential training for children. They must learn that "they were not to have any thing, because it pleased them, but because it was thought fit for them" (§38). We must not cater to their wants, but rather reason must operate in deciding what is good for them. A general rule of educating is that "the less Reason they have of their own, the more are they to be under the Absolute Power and Restraint of those, in whose Hands they are" (§39). Locke is not, as it may seem, urging obedience to the will of parents and tutors but to their reason. Although reason and desire are for the most part antithetical in Locke's concept of human nature (§52), he is not recommending that children be kept from pleasure and happiness but rather that what enjoyments they have should come "only as the Consequences of the State of Esteem and Acceptation" (§53).

To accomplish the control necessary for guiding children by reason, we need to use fear and awe in early years and friendship in later ones. Some passions can be useful in training the child. This combination of love and fear is said to be "the great Principle, whereby you will always have hold upon" your son, "to turn his Mind to the Ways of Vertue, and Honour" (§99). If properly cultivated, a son's reverence for his father can become as hard for the son to resist as "the Principles of his Nature" (§100). Love, fear, and awe are motives to action by which we can train and cultivate children's characters and behaviour. If we do not succeed in teaching or getting children to resist the demands of present pleasure and pain "for the sake of what Reason tells him is fit to be done", he will lack "the true Principle of Vertue and Industry" (§45).

We should be trying to motivate children to act out of love, virtue, and reputation. But these are acquired, not native (i.e. natural), motives for action (§42). For early training, the rod is not a good means for helping children to acquire these motives. In fact, use of the rod encourages, rather than prevents, the "Natural Propensity to indulge Corporal and present Pleasure, and to avoid Pain" (§48). If a child "drudges at his Book" and keeps from doing what he would like to do only out of fear of punishment, "he in this only preferrs the greater *Corporal Pleasure*, or avoids the greater *Corporal Pain*" (§48).Corporal punishment thus strengthens the kind of motives we should be trying to replace.[5] Similarly, we must avoid the opposite method of rewarding a child for good actions by giving him sweets or other pleasant things, since this method would "but authorize his Love of Pleasure" (§52). Such a method only reinforces his notion that the things he wants and that please him are what are to be sought.

Some readers of Locke feel that he was struggling between the poles of hedonism and rationalism in his account of moral man. It is clear that he considered knowledge of good, of what one ought to do, as an insufficient motive for one to act, unless one has been systematically guided and trained for many years. Therein lies the importance of education, whether it be in the family or by a tutor. The role of the affective side of man in this training process is stressed many times in the *Education*. The "only Motives to a rational Creature" are "Good and Evil, *Reward* and *Punishment*" (§54), the ultimate motive being fear of eternal punishment by God. Fear is "an Uneasiness under the

Apprehension of that coming upon us which we dislike" (§115). Dislike of evil is "so natural to Mankind, that no Body . . . can be without fear of it". He identifies "the two great Springs of Action" as "*Foresight* and *Desire*", meaning that the desire to avoid pain or evil and to gain pleasure or good, coupled with a knowledge of the consequences of action, is what motivates men to act. Desire must be put to the use of reason. These motives are "the Spur and Reins, whereby all Mankind are set on work" (§54). What is wrong with our usual handling of children is that we use the pleasure and pains of the body rather than pleasure and pains of the mind to spur children to action (§55). "*Esteem* and *Disgrace* are, of all others, the most powerful Incentives to the Mind" (§56); we act in accordance with reason, but we do so only if our motives are either fear of disgrace or love of esteem. As reinforcements for these psychological motives, Locke says that "other *agreeable or disagreeable Things should constantly accompany these different States*" (§58), but not as particular rewards or punishments for some particular action, rather as necessary accompaniments of the states of disgrace or commendation.

> In this way the Objects of their Desires are made assisting to Vertue; when a settled Experience from the beginning teaches Children, that the Things they delight in belong to, and are to be enjoyed by those only, who are in a State of Reputation. (§58; cf.78)

DOES THE MAN OR THE SOUL THINK

We began this chapter with a brief account of Locke's notion of man as a living, biological organization of nerves, muscles, brain, etc. In being an organization of matter with life, we share these traits with plants and animals. Where we differ is in having a host of psychological components, ranging from the innate practical principle of seeking pleasure and avoiding pain, to relatively fixed character traits or natural tempers, to desires and passions, to faculties producing ideational and cognitive content. The *Education* tells us how the tutor (as well as the parents) should work with all these natural features of human nature, guiding and training, harnessing the passions and emotions and using them to mould the child into a moral being. Moral man is in the first instance a being habituated to virtue, but in this habituation strives as well for understanding. The educative process starts with basic human nature and tries to overlay that nature with rationality, a rationality inherent in human nature but in danger of being obscured by the affective side of that nature. The process of education, of growing up in a family, is a progression from man to moral man. The goal is to bring into existence a responsible, self-conscious person.

The term 'person' is for us a very ordinary one, but for Locke it became a specialized and almost technical term. There are in the *Essay* some ordinary uses of that term (e.g. 1.3.3; 1.4.22; 2.25.5). Even the discussion of the question, "does the soul always think?", uses 'person' in the non-technical sense (2.1.9–21). This passage does, however, raise some of the questions and puzzlements which are elaborated in the later chapter on 'Identity and Diversity', where Locke presents his specialized sense of the term 'person'. What is interesting about this 2.1.9–21 passage is the way Locke presents the puzzlements about personal identity in the traditional language of "soul" as a metaphysical entity.

Perhaps with some Cartesians (who identified the essence of that which thinks as thought) in mind, Locke reformulates this doctrine as the opinion "that the Soul always thinks" (2.1.9). The essence of any thing, of any substance (so the doctrine went), is a property without which that thing cannot exist. Hence, if thought is the essence of that which thinks, that which thinks must always think. Descartes had talked of two substances, *res extensa* (body or matter) and *res cogitans* (mind or soul). Locke admits that "We know certainly by Experience, that we sometimes think, and thence draw this infallible Consequence, That there is something in us, that has a Power to think . . . ." (§10). The move from "we sometimes think" to "something in us thinks" is one Locke is not particularly comfortable with, but at this point he is not concerned to show the uncertainty and ambiguity of this notion of a thinking substance. The reader can, however, hardly miss the oddness Locke felt about the notion that not he, but something in him, thinks. He proceeds to use several *reductio* arguments in his attack against the notion that that which in us thinks does so always.

The absurdity of this claim about the soul always thinking lies in its divorce of the soul from the man. If the soul can think and be happy or sad, enjoy pleasure or suffer pain, while the body sleeps, the man is not conscious of those thoughts or states. The consequence would be that Socrates asleep and Socrates awake "is not the same Person", since the latter has "no Knowledge of, or Concernment for that Happiness, or Misery of his Soul" (§11). With the soul thus separated from the body and the man, Locke highlights the strangeness of a soul selecting "for its Scene of Thinking, the Body of another Man" (§12). The waking man and the sleeping man, or Castor and Pollux (to use his examples), share one soul between them. The soul is that which thinks, in the one man when he is awake, in the other when the first sleeps. The result is, Locke suggests rhetorically, clear:

> Whether *Castor* and *Pollux*, thus, with only one Soul between them, which thinks and perceives in one, what the other is never conscious of, nor is concerned for, are not two as distinct Persons, as *Castor* and *Hercules*; or, as *Socrates* and *Plato* were?

Those who claim the soul does the thinking, and that it does so always, "make the Soul and the Man two Persons" (§12), for "To suppose the Soul to think, and the Man not to perceive it, is . . . to make two Persons in one Man" (§19).

The many details of Locke's arguments for this conclusion need not detain us. What is important, besides this general conclusion of two persons in one man, is a theme woven through the details, the theme of the unity of mind and body. In section 11 of the *Essay*, Locke says it is worth considering (though he does not pause to do so) "whether sleeping without dreaming be not an Affection of the whole Man, Mind as well as Body". In another section, he suggests that the defenders of the claim that the soul always thinks might argue:

> that in a waking Man, the materials of the Body are employ'd, and made use of, in thinking; and that the memory of Thoughts, is retained by the impressions that are made on the Brain, and the traces there left after such thinking; but that in the *thinking of the Soul*, which is not perceived *in a sleeping Man*, there the Soul thinks apart, and *making no use* of the Organs of *the Body, leaves no impression on it, and consequently no memory* of such Thoughts. (§15)

He rejects this supposition because of his belief that "whatever *Ideas* the Mind can receive, and contemplate without the help of the Body, it is reasonable to conclude, it can retain without the help of the Body too" (§15). In a third passage, the same theme of the closeness between mind and body resurfaces. This time, the important property, for Locke, of rationality appears. Locke wants to know:

> Whether the Soul, when it thinks thus apart, and as it were separate from the Body, acts less rationally than when conjointly with it, or no; If its separate Thoughts be less rational, then these Men must say, That the Soul owes the perfection of rational thinking to the Body; . . . (§16)

In another passage, Locke suggests that either the soul "remembers something that the Man does not; or else that Memory belongs only to such *Ideas*, as are derived from the Body, or the Minds Operations about them" (§17). Finally, near the end of his discussion of this topic, Locke indicates his impatience with the notion that something in him thinks, when he throws off the passing remark: "that the humane Soul, or which is all one, that a Man always thinks" (§18).

The theme of the unity of mind and body introduced in this discussion of the question of what it is that thinks – the man or the soul – has suggested that the psychological features of man (memory, rationality, thoughts, ideas) are a function of both components. The characterization of man which we examined at the beginning of this chapter also linked the physiological features with the ideational and affective ones. In addition, Locke's account of man stressed the fact that our concept of man links the outward physical shape with these other features. It is not, he insists, "the *Idea* of a thinking or rational Being alone, that makes the *Idea* of a *Man* in most Peoples Sense; but of a Body so and so shaped joined to it . . ." (2.27.8).

Locke's account of man, especially of moral man, of the man trained to virtue by the educator, is not yet complete. That he wants to use the term "person" in a specialized sense is perhaps first indicated in *Essay* 2.27.7, where, speaking of the general concept of identity, he remarks that to explicate this concept we need only be clear about the referent of that word or idea. Does it stand for or refer to the same substance, the same man, or the same person? We know what 'same man' refers to and, from the discussion of whether the soul always thinks, we may guess that Locke's passing remark about the *man* being what thinks (and from the introduction there of the term 'person') will be elaborated and refined in his discussion of identity.

THE PERSON

In the chapter where Locke develops his specialized concept of the person, he remarks that "in the ordinary way of speaking, the same Person, and the same Man, stand for one and the same thing" (2.27.15). Locke finds it necessary to distinguish between man and person. What are his reasons for such a distinction, what does the distinction enable him to do which he could not have done with just the two notions of man and moral man? Near the end of his discussion of personal identity, Locke says that 'person' is "a Forensick Term appropriating Actions and their Merit" (§26). So that term has something to do with actions, with the ownership of those actions, and with their merit, their moral worth. Some of the other characteristics he uses to describe the self or person (these two terms tend to be used interchangeably) are also revealing of the answer to our question.

A person or self is an intelligent being, it reasons and reflects, it can consider itself the same over time and in different places (§9). A self or person is concerned for and sympathizes with its body and its parts (§11). A person is concerned for its actions and is accountable for them (§16). A person is "sensible of Happiness or Misery" and must grant that "there is something that is *himself*, that he is concerned for, and would have happy" (§25). A self is a conscious thinking thing "sensible, or conscious of Pleasure and Pain, capable of Happiness and Misery, and so is concern'd for it *self*, as far as that consciousness extends" (§17). A self owns its actions (§17), it is also "capable of a Law", meaning it is able to recognize and follow, or is subject to, moral laws, ultimately to God's laws. In the person and the identity of that person is founded "all the Right and Justice of Reward and Punishment" (§18).

When Locke raises in these passages some of those questions about two persons and one soul, he remarks first of all that same soul is really not relevant to same person: those terms refer to different items. The more important comment on this question of different persons in one soul is found in section 14. Suppose that a man today believes he has the same soul that was in Nestor or Thersites at the siege of Troy, but lacks any awareness of having been at Troy (which is the way this puzzle case was formulated). Locke asks: can that man really conceive himself to be the same person with either of those men? The test is, "Can he be concerned in either of their Actions? Attribute them to himself, or think them his own more than the Actions of any other Man, that ever existed?"

What this example and Locke's comment on it reveals is that 'person' refers to a man who can take responsibility for his actions and who is concerned with those actions and their consequences, a man who is vitally interested in his moral worth and his happiness, and who recognizes he is God's workmanship. It is the concern – the moral, responsible concern – taken for what he does which Locke stresses in his depiction of a person. After the educator has successfully trained the child to act rationally and virtuously, the child must learn to accept responsibility for his actions. A moral man becomes a person when he learns to act intentionally, out of deliberation over right and good, in respect of moral laws which are or are ultimately based upon God's law.

Another way to bring out what Locke is saying is to remark that one cannot act responsibly and morally by chance, unconsciously, or just out of habit. One's actions when performed in any of these ways can of course have moral consequences, but the child who behaves according to virtue does not act virtuously unless and until that child acts self-consciously with a full understanding of right and wrong, and with a clear recognition that those actions are his actions. A formula used by Locke to emphasize the importance of the sense of self and self-ownership needed for responsible moral action is to say that a person "can consider it self as it self, the same thinking thing in different times and places" (§9). The means by which a person acquires this sense of self is the awareness or consciousness which is inseparable from thinking. While Locke rejects the claim that we or our soul always thinks, he insists that we cannot think without being aware that we are thinking, where 'thinking' covers the whole range of acts of awareness. It is impossible "for any one to perceive, without perceiving, that he does perceive. When we see, hear, smell, taste, feel, meditate, or will any thing, we know that we do so" (§9). When I perceive in any of these modes, I know that I am seeing, hearing, believing, etc.; I know or am aware that it is I who am perceiving. The act of reflective awareness which accompanies all modes of awareness gives me my sense of self. Those acts of perceiving are owned, they are mine, not yours. There can be no ownerless acts of thinking, willing, believing, seeing. Any of these acts can be and often are ascribed to a person by another: I speak of your beliefs, your intentions, I say you looked but did not see, you desired to do good. These third-person ascriptions sometimes fit, at other times fail to fit, the person to whom they are ascribed.

Such third-person ascriptions are intended to be ascribed to the *person*, but our access to that person is only through the *man*, through the behaviour, including linguistic behaviour, of the man. The educator, or parents (friends as well) do become adept at making person-ascriptions on the basis of what they observe. Locke does not want to raise any questions about scepticism here: can we really know another person? His point throughout 2.27 is to emphasize that 'person' is properly a first-person term. *I* come by my concept of person through *my* acts of perceiving, including the act of being aware that *I* am perceiving. Moreover, if I am to accept full responsibility for what I do, I *must* have that awareness of what I have done, know that those acts were mine. It is this first-person awareness of my actions which is the basis of moral responsibility. That awareness, too, constitutes my identity as a person, my personal identity, my *"personal self"* (§11). A self can only be personal.

Confronting the question, if immaterial substances (i.e. souls) are what thinks, can the same person survive a change of substance, Locke points out that we cannot answer this question until (a) we know more about the nature of such thinking substances, and (b) we know "whether the consciousness of past Actions can be transferr'd from one thinking Substance to another" (§13). The answer would be easy for (b) if 'same consciousness' meant the "same individual Action" that happened in the past. But if the same consciousness (that is, my awareness of my past actions) is "a present representation of a past Action" (as Locke means to use that phrase), the answer is more difficult, especially if we demand to *know* that my awareness of some action, my sense of owning specific actions, may be false. In the face of that possibility, Locke resolves the issue into the goodness of God, "who as far as the Happiness or Misery of any of his sensible Creatures is concerned in it, will not by a fatal Error of theirs transfer from one to another, that consciousness, which draws Reward or Punishment with it" (§13). He was confident that "no one shall be made to answer for what he knows nothing of" (§22).

The appeal to the goodness of God is not just an easy way around a difficult theoretical question. That appeal reveals an important feature of Locke's concept of person and of morality, and of the eschatological consequences. The ascription of praise and blame (in particular, of eternal rewards and punishments) requires that the person recognize that he is rewarded or punished for what *he* has done. It is almost a conceptual truth for Locke that we can only hold a person responsible for the action he has performed and has recognized as his own. This is the meaning of the Apostle's words, "that at the Great Day, when every one shall *receive according to his doings, the secrets of all Hearts shall be laid open*" (§26). The sentence on that judgement day

shall be justified by the consciousness all Persons shall have, that they *themselves* in what Bodies soever they appear, or what Substances soever that consciousness adheres to, are the *same*, that committed those Actions, and deserve that Punishment for them. (§26)

A person, then, is that rational, intelligent, concerned, rule-following being who acts in the world and who is conscious of those actions as his. The person or self is constituted by the actions he performs and by the awareness he has of those actions as his. It is the awareness that I have of my actions, past and present, that makes them the actions of the person I am.

Nothing but consciousness can unite remote Existences into the same Person, the Identity of substance will not do it. For whatever Substance there is, however framed, without consciousness, there is no Person: And a Carcase may be a Person, as well as any sort of Substance be so without consciousness. (§23)

More precisely,

> as far as any intelligent Being can repeat the *Idea* of any past
> Action with the same consciousness it had of it at first, and with
> the same consciousness it has of any present Action; so far it is the
> same *personal self*. (§10)

The phrase, "with the same consciousness it has of any present
Action" clearly means 'with the consciousness of that action
being mine'. The uniting by this awareness or consciousness of
the actions I have done is similar, Locke remarks, to the way one
continuous life unites different particles of matter into *one* plant
or animal. It is my consciousness that appropriates thoughts and
actions, makes them my own: "whatever past Actions it cannot
reconcile or appropriate to that present *self* by consciousness, it
can be no more concerned in, than if they had never been done:
. . ." (§26).

This appropriating consciousness is not just memory, not just a
matter of recalling some thought or action, although memory *is*
involved for past actions and thoughts. The aspect of memory
that is involved by the appropriating consciousness is
characterized by Locke in an earlier discussion of memory as "a
consciousness that it [the idea] had been there before, and was
not wholly a Stranger to the mind" (1.4.20). If an idea comes into
the mind without that consciousness of its having been there
before, it comes there not by memory. But this consciousness of
"a former acquaintance" is only part of the appropriating
consciousness so crucial for the constituting of a person. The
other components in the appropriating consciousness are those of
being concerned for the deeds I have done, concerned for their
happiness-producing, for their moral worth, for their importance
in my intentional actions. To own something, whether an action,
a piece of land, or a self, is to be proud of or feel guilty for that
possession, to take responsibility for and be accountable for it.
All of these qualities are ingredients in that appropriating
consciousness by means of which I become a person with a
character and a history.

NOTES

1 Reprinted in *The Educational Writings of John Locke*, James L.
Axtell (1968), p. 421.

2 *Conduct of the Understanding*, §2, in *Works* (1823 edn) vol. III, p. 207.
3 *Ibid.*, §3, p. 209.
4 *Ibid.*, §4, p. 215.
5 *Ibid.*, §30, p. 259.

2

Moral Rules and Standards

Locke's distinction between man, moral man and person is portrayed in his account of the education of a child. The educator starts with a living organism already possessed of faculties, traits, natural tempers and passions. The education process gradually moulds the child into a moral agent, first by habituating him to virtuous behaviour and attitudes, and then by leading him to a rational understanding of the responsibilities we all have for our actions as persons. Where does the tutor turn to discover the standards of rationality and virtue? There is in Locke's writing a double approach to this question, both approaches reflecting two important sides of his thought and character. The one approach is to pull out God's injunctions from passages in the Bible. The other is to discover moral laws by using the faculty of reason. The first testifies to Locke's fundamental commitment to Christianity, the second indicates his equally strong commitment to reason and rationality.

MORAL EDUCATION

According to Locke, the proper development of the natural faculties of mind is an important function of education, but that development depends upon prior habituation to virtue. In an early statement of *Some Thoughts concerning Education* we are given the main aim of education in Locke's view: to work into children's nature "the Principles and Practices of Vertue, and good Breeding" (§70, 94). The relation between virtue and the proper exercise of our faculties, especially of reason, reveals the very roots of Locke's view of human nature and the concept of action. Moral rules for Locke are either laws of nature or derivations from those laws. Discovery of the laws of nature can be made by reading the Scriptures; he recommends that children read parts of the Bible for, among other things, the moral rules "scattered up and down" in it (§159). But laws of nature (and hence moral rules as well) are also laws of reason. Reason is the voice of God in man. Whether or not the laws of nature can be discovered by reason alone (as Locke sometimes claimed), the moral man is one who comes to understand the rationality of those rules: to be moral is to be rational. The law of nature or reason binds all men, but children do not acquire that obligation until they acquire the use of reason: "no Body can be under a Law, which is not promulgated to him; and the Law being promulgated or made known by *Reason* only, he that is not come to the Use of his *Reason*, cannot be said to be *under this Law*."[1]

Locke's comments on children, rationality, obligation and moral law occur in the context of a doctrine about the rights of children and the duties of parents toward them. This doctrine is itself underlaid by a notion about the natural inclinations parents have toward the well-being of their children. In saying that *"Hatred* or *Love*, to Beings capable of Happiness or Misery, is often the Uneasiness or Delight, which we find in our selves arising from a consideration of their very Being or Happiness", Locke offers as an example, "the Being and Welfare of a Man's Children or Friends, producing constant Delight in him" (*Essay*, 2.20.5). In his *Two Treatises of Government* Locke says that parents are "taught by Natural Love and Tenderness to provide" for their children. He explains that "God hath woven into the Principles of Humane Nature such a tenderness for their Off-Spring" (TII:67). Preservation of the young is, in fact, a rule that nature teaches all animals (TI:56). Locke's dispute with Sir Robert Filmer arose primarily because Filmer had tried to argue that the power and dominion of Adam over his offspring was the model for and origin of political power.[2] Locke found many faults with Filmer's argument but he insisted that *"Begetting of Children makes them not Slaves to their Fathers"* (TI:51). The power of the magistrate over a subject differs in kind from the power of a father over his children (TII:2). In fact, "A *Child is born a*

Subject of no Country or Government" (TII:118). He makes that choice only when he reaches the age of reason.

The father–son or parent–child relation (and Locke had to point out to Filmer that the Bible makes both parents responsible for the children) is not one of power but one of love regulated by inclinations that God gives to each person to love his or her children. The parent–child relation also has some rights and duties pertaining to it, prescribed by the law of nature. More than once in Locke's writings, natural inclinations are linked with rights. In *Two Treatises* self-preservation is both an inclination we all have and a right. The *Education* links love and duty: "They love their little ones, and 'tis their Duty" (34). "Honour thy Father and Mother" is an eternal law prescribing this parent–child relation (TI:64). Children have a right to inherit the goods and possessions of their parents; that right is one aspect of the natural law that says parents must provide for their children (TI:88). The correlative right for children is that they should be "nourished and maintained by their Parents" (*ibid.*). In these passages Locke was speaking specifically of "Possessions and Commodities of Life valuable by Money", not of "that Reverence, Acknowledgement, Respect and Honour that is always due from Children to their Parents" (TI:90). A man also has a right to be cared for and maintained by his children when he needs it. In contrast to Filmer, Locke emphasized that: "All that a Child has a Right to claim from his Father is Nourishment and Education, and the things nature furnishes for the support of Life: But he has no Right to demand *Rule* and *Dominion* from him" (TI:93). Locke also points out that "a Father cannot alien the Power he has over his Child, he may perhaps to some degree forfeit it, but cannot transfer it" (TI:100). Locke addressed this passage to incompetent or indifferent parents.

Locke's concepts of freedom and law linked them together: a lawless man is not free. "For *Law* in its true Notion, is not so much the Limitation as *the direction of a free and intelligent Agent* to his proper Interest" (TII:57). The virtuous man is a free man. The child is an apprentice to freedom and reason. All men are equal in respect to jurisdiction and dominion one over another: each has a natural right (derived from a law of nature) to his freedom without being subjected to the will of another (TII:54). While children are not born in "the full State of *Equality*", they are nevertheless born to it (TII:55). The natural right children have for tuition and guidance gives parents the obligation to educate their children. "He that *understands* for him, must *will* for him too; he must prescribe to his Will, and regulate his Actions" (TII:58). After the child has reached the age of reason, he is free and equal; "after that, the Father and Son are equally *free* as much as Tutor and Pupil after Nonage" (TII:59). Age and education generally bring reason and the ability to govern oneself. Exactly when this happens is, Locke quotes Richard Hooker as saying, *"more easie for sense to discern, than for any one by Skill and Learning to determine"* (TII:61). One of the criteria for the age of reason is being able to understand "that Law he is to govern himself by", meaning the law of nature or reason. Parental power is

> nothing but that, which Parents have over their Children, to govern them for the Childrens good, till they come to the use of Reason, or a state of Knowledge, wherein they may be supposed capable to understand that Rule, whether it be the Law of Nature, or the municipal Law of their Country they are to govern themselves by. (TII:170)

To guide one's self by the law of nature and reason is not merely to live an orderly and virtuous life: it is to have the very essence of humanity. To turn the child

> loose to an unrestrain'd Liberty, before he has Reason to guide him, is not the allowing him the priviledge of his Nature, to be free; but to thrust him out amongst Brutes, and abandon him to a state as wretched, and as much beneath that of a Man, as theirs. (TII:63)

Education literally humanizes the child by bringing him to reason and virtue, the defining marks of man.

Locke's suggestion that the incorrect use of liberty puts the child "out amongst Brutes" was no idle metaphor. *Two Treatises* confirms the importance and seriousness for Locke of rationality differentiating men from brutes, a rationality that gives us laws of nature as the framework for freedom. The transgressor of the laws of nature has in effect declared "himself to live by another Rule, than that of reason and common Equity" (TII:8). Such persons are "noxious things" which may be destroyed if means cannot be found to make them repent. A man who renounces reason by failing to act in accordance with its laws declares "War against all Mankind, and therefore may be destroyed as a *Lyon* or a *Tyger*, one of those wild Savage Beasts, with whom Men can have no Society nor Security" (TII:11). The significance of Locke's training for virtue in his *Education* is enhanced when we keep in mind these strong views expressed in his political writings on what could be termed "moral monsters". Presumably even these persons who transgress the laws of nature would still meet the definition of a person, their consciousness would appropriate the thoughts and actions which they had and had performed. But the forensic side of Locke's concept of person reminds us that a person is responsible for his actions. For anyone who flouts the laws of nature, for one who violates the civil laws of society which are founded on the law of nature, the appropriating consciousness has intentionally acted against the law. In that way, such a person for Locke ceases to be a person, at least ceases to be a moral agent. We should resist the temptation to view Locke's account of personal identity as being merely an analytical device for dealing with identity. It is instead a serious attempt to characterize moral identity.

Seen in this light, Locke's insistence that the main goal of education is the cultivation of virtue and good manners is no mere echo of similar emphases in other educational writings of that time. Locke has firmly linked his ethical doctrine with his views on education in a way that enables us to see the place of the *Education* in his general view of man and person. He does present some suggestions for teaching particular subjects to children, but the study of specific subject matter is subordinated to the acquisition of virtue. Becoming a responsible person is of fundamental importance.

There is a sense in which virtue cannot be taught. To some extent Locke is laying down an ideal, though the various techniques he cites suggest how children can be brought to have and to use the ordinary virtues, along with justice, generosity, sobriety, and industry. Education as an art must replace education as facts and rules to be memorized. One of the main faults in "the ordinary Method of Education" was "The Charging of Children's Memories, upon all Occasions, with *Rules* and

Precepts, which they often do not understand, and constantly as soon forget as given" (*Education*, §64). Not only the example of those around them is important in instilling virtuous actions: the child should be encouraged to repeat the action that is to be developed so that the tutor or parent "may Correct what is indecent or constrain'd in it, till it be perfected into an habitual and becoming Easiness" (§66). It is by reiterated actions that virtue and manners can be acquired (§67).

Neither rules nor abstract reasoning will by themselves succeed in teaching virtue. Locke, in this ancient debate, is careful to emphasize that in cultivating the proper habits, adults should treat children as rational beings. We should give them reasons for the actions we praise or blame, but only such reasons "as their Age and Understanding are capable of, and those proposed always *in* very *few and plain Words*" (§81). In fact, Locke assures us that children "love to be treated as Rational Creatures sooner than is imagined"; one way to do this is to let them see that what we ourselves do is not done out of passion or fancy (§81). The task of developing "the physiognomy of the mind" is to ensure that the mind or the person is on all occasions "disposed to consent to nothing, but what may be suitable to the Dignity and Excellency of a rational Creature" (§31). Rationality has to be achieved within the framework of our fixed character traits and despite our desires and wants.

REASON AND MORAL TRUTHS

With the great importance given to virtue and moral education, Locke must have held firm convictions about the nature of moral truths and about ways to discover them. It is clear that for him, moral truths, the standards for right action, are founded on, if not derived from, God's laws. The true touchstone for morality is, he says in the *Essay*, "the *Divine* Law" (2.28.8). Moral truths are not exhausted by God's explicit injunctions, however. Some moral truths, or certain aspects of those truths, are self-evident. The similarities between reason as the source of such systemic truths as are found in mathematics or geometry and reason as the source of some aspects of truths in morality, led Locke to suggest that reason could construct demonstrations of moral truths, after the same fashion as Euclid did in geometry.

In a demonstration, what we do is to link one notion to another in such a way that the conclusion can be seen to be true. What the demonstrator does is to try various techniques in order to help you understand the proposition and its relations to other propositions. The connecting ideas, those that enable us to see how other ideas about, e.g., a triangle are related, are called "intervening *Ideas*". When our understanding apprehends the relations between the angles of a triangle and some other property, and when it grasps this relation clearly, there we have demonstration (*Essay*, 4.2.3). The more traditional notion of demonstration links it with deduction, placing the emphasis upon the relation between propositions, as if those relations hold whether anyone perceives them or not. The notion of demonstration in Descartes and Locke locates the demonstration with the success in understanding. Intellectual seeing, immediate understanding, or intuition operates at each stage of a demonstration, for we must grasp and understand each of the steps. Reason guides the mind through the steps, but it is the understanding which apprehends the connections and perceives the truth of the conclusion. The faculty of understanding operates in apprehending all truths, whether *truths of the world* or truths in mathematics and geometry. The truths Locke discusses when explicating demonstration are not extracted from the world by observation, although those, as well as moral truths, do have application to the world and to human action.

Locke characterizes mathematical truths as referring to our ideas only, not to the world, but he does not mean to deny that they can have application to the world. Newton was soon to demonstrate that fact in dramatic ways. The aspect of these truths Locke wants to stress, in saying they refer to ideas only, is the way in which they serve as definitions. The properties of a triangle are specified by our ideas, our concepts, our definitions, not by objects in the world. Our idea of gold, on the other hand, or of the behaviour of bodies, must be derived from examining gold and bodies carefully. From the defined properties of a triangle, certain truths follow, whether there is in the world any triangular object or not. The definition or idea of a triangle sets the standard for triangular objects, if there happen to be any.

All the Discourses of the Mathematicians about the squaring of a Circle, conick Sections, or any other part of Mathematicks, *concern not* the *Existence* of any of those Figures: but their Demonstrations, which depend on their *Ideas*, are the same, whether there be any Square or Circle existing in the World, or no. (*Essay,* 4.4.8)

Such an idea is what Locke calls an *archetype*, a standard or model.

In similar way, he wants to say that moral ideas (and action concepts in general) are also archetypes. The parallel passage for moral ideas explains Locke's meaning:

In the same manner [as in geometry], the Truth and Certainty of *moral* Discourses abstracts from the Lives of Men, and the Existence of those Vertues in the World, whereof they treat: Nor are *Tully's* Offices less true, because there is no Body in the world that exactly practices his Rules, and lives up to that pattern of a vertuous Man, which he has given us, and which existed no where, when he writ, but in *Idea*. (*Essay*, 4.4.8)[3]

It is because archetype ideas set the standard to be followed by anything which is an instance of them, that we can reach a certainty in mathematical and moral knowledge not possible in our knowledge of the world. Scientific knowledge depends upon the world and upon our finding out how the world is. Mathematical and moral knowledge depend only upon ideas, and the relations between those ideas.

Locke is quick to point out that this view of moral truths does not leave it open for each of us to define justice, for example, as we please. At least, defining the action, what counts as justice, is not open to such relativism, although of course we may change the words around and still have the same idea or concept. Nor does Locke mean to say that the person, the moral agent, is the author and touchstone of right and wrong. His notion of moral truths and of their possible demonstration is somewhat obscure. It is offered in the general context of Christian morality. It has sometimes been taken as an alternative to seeking God's laws. It would be more correct to say that demonstration is a way, could it be made, of understanding some of the inter-relations between moral concepts. Four examples offered by Locke will help illustrate what he had in mind in characterizing moral ideas as archetypes, and in suggesting that one could demonstrate how those ideas are related.

(a) Just as terms such as 'trapezoid', 'equilateral', or 'rectangular' have fixed meanings, so with the term 'justice'. That we all agree on the meaning of 'justice' is illustrated by supposing "a Man have the *Idea* of taking from others, without their Consent, what their honest Industry has possessed them of, and call this *Justice*" (4.4.9). Changing the words will not change the relations holding between those ideas. Seeing the conceptual connections between the ideas of 'taking from others', 'without their consent', etc., is to understand what injustice is.

(b) If we have an idea of "a supreme Being, infinite in Power, Goodness, and Wisdom, whose Workmanship we are, and on whom we depend", and if we have an idea of "our selves, as understanding, rational Beings", we ought to be able to discover the "Foundations of our Duty and Rules of Action" (4.3.18). The moral truth here is that being the workmanship of a God who has those properties, we can understand that we ought to follow his rules.

(c) Another moral truth intuited or grasped through conceptual connections concerns justice again. "*Where there is no Property, there is no Injustice.*" This proposition is as "certain as any Demonstration in *Euclid*". The way to this conclusion is indicated by Locke:

> For the *Idea* of *Property*, being a right to any thing; and the *Idea* to which the Name *Injustice* is given, being the Invasion or Violation of that right; it is evident, that these *Ideas* being thus established, and these Names annexed to them, I can as certainly know this Proposition to be true, as that a Triangle has three Angles equal to two right ones. (*ibid.*)

(d) Another moral truth about which we can be as certain as of any mathematical truth is: "*No Government allows absolute Liberty.*" The conceptual connections leading to this proposition are as follows: "The *Idea of* Government being the establishment of Society upon certain Rules or Laws, which require Conformity to them; and the *Idea* of absolute Liberty being for any one to do whatever he pleases" (4.3.18). The understanding perceives the incompatibility between this latter idea and the former.

Whatever we may think of these examples, the point Locke is making is clear: it ought to be possible to start in morality with some ideas whose meaning is clear, to use our reason to trace out the relations these ideas have to each other. In that way, we ought to be able, by reason alone, to discover or understand moral truths. The programme was bold. Locke did not, even after several friends urged him to do so, complete it. We can conjecture why he did not and could not complete his suggestion in quite the form in which he thought possible.

We need to ask, what would guide our selection of ideas to serve as guides for action? How would I know which ideas contain moral content and stand in moral relations to what other ideas? The answer seems fairly clear: I acquire those ideas from my education and from my society. Acquiring and understanding the ideas which contain moral content is part of the socialization process. The examples cited above are conceptual truths, once we are in possession of the ideas in those examples. To govern requires rules on how to govern. Rules must be followed. But this example does not tell us what rules a government should have or whether, in the case of example (c), property and its protection should be part of government and its rules. Example (b) is a conceptual truth just because of the idea of the workman and his product, but we do not know from that example the specific ways in which God is to be obeyed. The workmanship model is an important one for Locke. It shows us that his moral ideas are located in a religious, indeed a Christian framework. When, in his *Reasonableness of Christianity*, Locke says that what reason might have been able to discover on its own has been revealed to us in the Bible and in the life of Christ, we see where it is that we have to look to fill out the conceptual truths.[4] It is much less controversial to say that what has been revealed is reasonable, that reasons can be given for the moral rules of Christianity. But how specific is the Bible and the life of Christ, or how specific was Locke, in identifying moral rules and standards?

Locke has distinguished two kinds of truths, *truths of the world* and *systemic truths*. The first kind depend for their truth on the world. The second depend upon the system to which they belong, whether it be the system of Euclidean geometry or the system of the Christian religion. To discover the truth of a claim about the world requires that we use experience and observation, aided in more complex science by hypotheses and reasoning. To discover a systemic truth, we need only use reason alone, either to get clear about the ideas and concepts involved in the claim or to trace out the connections between those ideas and concepts. The two examples Locke uses of systemic truths are geometrical and moral truths.

Systemic truths lay down standards which anything in the world must meet if it is to be an instance of, e.g., a triangle or a square, an act of murder or of homicide. It was this standard- and norm-setting aspect of systemic truths that Locke had in mind in using the word 'archetype'. The fixing of standards – for admission to a University or club, for playing a game, for winning a competition, for being the best of breed or show – all of these are familiar to us. We set ourselves standards which we do not always reach. Thus, *being a standard* does not require that there exist anything that exactly meets that standard. We can and often do rank a person's performance in terms of how close it came to the standard. Even the best of breed may have some faults. Thus, we can understand how standards are useful for assessing performances, even where the standard may be the ideal and never fully reached. But how do we go about setting up such standards? In the case of dog shows, standards are set on the basis of biological and genetic structures. We do not expect the ears or coat of a West Highland terrier to be like those of a poodle. We also set those standards with some notion of how each type of dog behaves – for example, as a hunter – and also with some regard to its 'natural' look when working or walking. In this case, we do not set standards in isolation from the dogs we are going to judge.

Are Locke's remarks about moral standards made in isolation from the nature of people? Human nature for Locke is a combination of reason and emotion. Children cannot be taught virtue, cannot even be trained for virtue, by just appealing to their reason and intellect. The goal Locke sets is for reason to control inclination, but the educator achieves this by working within the natural character of the child. Within Locke's theological and religious context, did he believe God laid down moral standards for judging people without reference to the nature of persons, without reference to human nature? While Locke does not answer this question directly, we can say that the faculty of reason which receives so much stress in his writings *is* the basis for the moral standards which we should follow. God's laws are reasonable and available to our reason. In order to decide whether the label 'reasonable' is anything more than a device, to decide whether Locke provides us with any criteria for determining what is reasonable, we need to examine what he says about laws of nature, God's laws, or laws of reason.

REASON AS NATURAL REVELATION

The word 'reason' has, Locke remarks, many different significations in the English language. The signification he gives to it differs from the usual ones: it stands for a faculty of man, a faculty "whereby Man is supposed to be distinguished from Beasts, and wherein it is evident he much surpasses them" *Essay*, 4.17.1). This specification of the meaning of 'reason' occurs in a chapter in which Locke attacks the traditional notion of formal, syllogistic reasoning. Reason as a faculty of the mind is not dependent upon syllogisms and rules for deriving conclusions from premises. These are *artificial* aids to that faculty. Locke stresses the *naturalness* of this faculty. It is given to all of us by God for our use; we have an obligation to use it and to use it well. The naturalness of this faculty is brought out in a striking fashion when Locke discusses the role of reason and faith in religious beliefs. Writing against the 'enthusiasts' (the fundamentalists of his day) who abandon reason for revelation, Locke says that "*Reason* is natural *Revelation*, whereby the eternal Father of Light, and Fountain of all Knowledge communicated to Mankind that portion of Truth, which he has laid within the reach of their natural Faculties" (*Essay*, 4.19.4). In its turn, revelation is characterized as "natural *Reason* enlarged by a new set of Discoveries communicated by GOD immediately, which *Reason* vouches the Truth of, by the Testimony and Proofs it gives, that they come from GOD."

The notion of reason as natural revelation had been developed much earlier in Locke's career, when in 1664 he was appointed Moral Censor at Christ Church. The lectures he gave in that capacity were never published in Locke's lifetime.[5] In those essays, Locke presented an account of the way reason, working with sense experience, comes to the recognition of specific truths about the existence of God and his laws. One feature of this account is the close similarity between the doctrine of the law of nature accepted by Locke and the claims for innate truths which he so strongly rejected in his 1690 *Essay concerning Human Understanding*. There were many writers in seventeenth-century England who accepted and defended a doctrine of innate knowledge and truth.[6] Often, the language they used was florid and literal-sounding: talk of a truth 'stampt' and its 'characters' indelibly written in the hearts of men, of 'red letters', or 'heavenly beams of light'. Examples of truths said to be innate in this way are: 'there is a god', 'God is powerful', 'promises are to be kept', 'parents are to be honoured'. This terminology and the examples were used by many writers in the century, even where they were attacking the doctrine. Locke was not the first to attack that doctrine, but his discussion is by far the most systematic and exhaustive. When the language was not so vivid and literal-sounding, writers said the test for innateness was the ready and prompt assent given to such truths once they are presented to us. Henry More, one of the Cambridge Platonists, used this more conservative language when defending innate knowledge.[7] Nathaniel Culverwel's language is less conservative but he expressly linked that doctrine with the law of nature. "There are stampt and printed upon the being of man, some cleare and undelible Principles, some first and Alphabetical Notions; by putting together of which it can spell out the Law of Nature."[8] Culverwel stressed the activity and spontaneity of the soul in the generation of its ideas and in its ready and immediate assent to certain moral and speculative principles. Some truths were said to be implicit in man, waiting to be recognized once the light of reason has been turned upon them: a kind of dispositional notion of innateness. The appeal to self-evident truths, particularly moral truths, was everywhere felt to be necessary for the preservation of morality. Morality in this way could be given an objective foundation, even though moral truths were, on this view of innateness, somehow 'in' man.

What Locke was doing in his polemic against the more extreme language of the account of innateness was to organize the various objections in such a way that the adherents to the doctrine would be led to spell out in precise terms just what they were claiming. He argued, in effect, that either the theory asserts something which not only is odd but which can never be verified, or that the theory (in its more conservative formulation) states an obvious fact about man, namely, that some truths are recognized as self-evident once we have acquired the mature use of our rational faculty. Locke's polemic was perhaps more directed against the flamboyant formulations, but his criticism of the conservative formulation was equally firm. Locke himself used the notion of 'the light of reason'. Reason is, as we are seeing, a very important faculty for him. What reason discovers is not innate, even though reason is natural revelation.

Locke was not unmindful that his polemic against innate knowledge might be interpreted as an attack upon the law of nature. He expressly warns against such an interpretation.

> There is a great deal of difference between an innate Law, and a Law of Nature; between something imprinted on our Minds in their very original, and something that we being ignorant of may attain to the knowledge of, by the use and due application of our natural Faculties. (1.3.13)

The law of nature and the dispositional version of innateness are clearly linked together. We can see this connection especially in the early *Essays on the Law of Nature*. Locke claims there that all knowledge comes either by inscription, tradition, or sense experience. A synonym for law of nature is right reason, "to which everyone who considers himself a human being lays claim" (p. 111; cf. pp. 135,213). The distinction in this remark between men of reason who are human beings proper and those others not yet at the age of reason (e.g. children) was a frequent one in the literature on innate principles. The dispositional test for innateness reappears in Locke's criterion for the law of nature in a passage from these early *Essays*.

> We do not maintain that this law of nature, written as it were on tablets, lies open in our hearts, and that, as soon as some inward light comes near it (like a torch approaching a notice board hung up in darkness), it is at length read, perceived, and noted by the rays of that light. Rather, by saying that something can be known by the light of nature, we mean nothing else but that there is some sort of truth to the knowledge of which a man can attain by himself and without the help of another, if he makes proper use of the faculties he is endowed with by nature. (p. 123)

Such a criterion as this can be made to include almost any truth, particularly those truths deemed necessary for morality. The law of nature for Locke plays the same role in morality as the appeal to innateness did for his contemporaries: it furnishes a firm and unalterable foundation for moral goodness. What he was arguing for in the second of these *Essays* was that the law of nature (what could be termed the 'moral rule') is not known through inscription or handed down by tradition but is known by reason through sense experience. He pretends, that is, to offer an experiential foundation for the moral rule, in radical opposition to the believers in its innate basis. But how precisely do the senses and reason work to produce the apprehension of the law of nature?

He argues first of all that, "If man makes use properly of his reason and of the inborn faculties with which nature has equipped him, he can attain to the knowledge of this law without any teacher instructing him in his duties . . ." (p. 127). From the appearances of sense perception, "reason and the power of arguing . . . advance to the notion of the maker" of nature (p. 133). Just as soon as man has the idea of God, "the notion of a universal law of nature binding on all men necessarily emerges". Reason and sense are the sole foundations for all knowledge. It is only these two faculties which "teach and educate the minds of men and . . . provide what is characteristic of the light of nature" (p. 147).

There are many assumptions contained in Locke's inference from sense experience to God and from that to God as a lawmaker, and thence to a law of nature. But the important point is not that his inferences rest upon unexpressed assumptions. What is important for us to notice is that the concept of reason for Locke is not the usual discursive faculty employed in drawing conclusions. Rather, it is reason as the light of nature, as natural revelation, which apprehends, more like immediate than mediate inference, on the basis of sensory material, the law or laws of nature. The revelations of this natural faculty are of the utmost importance for morality and religion. Locke was seeking to justify a system of morality by grounding the moral law in something objective. The law of nature is a decree of God, not of man's reason. It is part of God's will.

The precise relation between the law of nature, positive law, and the rules for ethical actions is not always clear from what Locke says. The doctrine of the law of nature contains the body of rules or precepts necessary for making individual and social action moral. What makes them rational seems mainly to be that they are discovered by reason, but the term 'rational' or 'reason' clearly contains praiseworthy connotations for Locke. A listing of some of the rules he claims in various passages as knowable by the light of reason strongly suggests that the moral rules which compose the law of nature could not be derived in any form, demonstrative or otherwise, from a single general law.

The light of reason or nature not only knows that there is a God who is supreme lawmaker; it knows very specific rules as derivable from the law of nature. The following rules (a fair sample) are taken from the early *Essays* and the second of his *Two Treatises*.

1. Love and respect and worship God (*Essays*, p. 195).
2. Obey your superiors (*ibid.*, p. 129).
3. Tell the truth and keep your promises (*ibid.*).
4. Be mild and pure of character and be friendly (*ibid.*).
5. Do not offend or injure, without cause, any person's health, life, or possessions (*ibid.*, p. 163;TII:6).
6. Be candid and friendly in talking about other people (*ibid.*).
7. Do not kill or steal (*ibid.*).
8. Love your neighbour and your parents (*ibid.*).
9. Console a distressed neighbour (*ibid.*).
10. Feed the hungry (*ibid.*).
11. "Whoso sheddeth man's blood, by man shall his blood be shed" (TII:11).
12. That property is mine which I have acquired through my labour, so long as I can use it before it spoils (TII:29–30).
13. Parents are to preserve, nourish, and educate their children (TII:56).

It is clearly impossible to derive these precepts from any single principle, whether it be innate, the light of reason, or a standard agreed upon by men. What these rules do is to disclose the moral framework in terms of which Locke examined society and civil government. Some of them are the same rules which his contemporaries claimed to be innate. All of them perform the same function as the principles said to be innate: they provide the moral foundation for his views on individual and social action.

Just as the line of argument for those who believed in innate ideas was that certain moral rules are correct because they are innate, so Locke's main defence for any moral rule is to say it is known to be true by the light of reason, that it is a law of nature. He nowhere formulates a general maxim which he calls 'the law of nature'. The law of nature turns out to be a list of laws or rules, all of which are apparent to the rational being, that is, to an individual trained in Locke's educational system and growing up in his civil society. These laws find their justification in God, as being God's will. Locke's general Christian framework is manifested again in his concept of reason and moral laws. What reason as natural revelation reveals is pretty much what any Christian can find in Jesus's example or in passages of the Bible.

NOTES

1 *Two Treatises of Government*, II:57.
2 Robert Filmer's *Patriarcha* (1680).
3 Tully is M. Tullius Cicero.
4 See *Works* (1823 edn), vol. VII, pp. 10–15.
5 There have been edited and published by W. von Leyden as *Essays on the Law of Nature* (1954).
6 For details, see my *John Locke and the Way of Ideas* (1956).
7 See his *Antidote against Atheisme* (1653).
8 *An Elegant and Learned Discourse of the Light of Nature* (1652), p. 54.

3

The Individual Socialized

In a discussion of moral relations, Locke remarks that the terms 'virtue' and 'vice' are "attributed only to such actions, as in each Country and Society are in reputation or discredit" (*Essay*, 2.28.10). Praise or blame, "by a secret and tacit consent establishes it self in the several Societies, Tribes, and Clubs of Men in the World"; it identifies virtue or vice in those societies and also serves as the goad for all persons to seek the one and avoid the other. Conceptually, reference to a rule or law determines which actions are morally right, determines the ends, objects, manners and circumstances of those actions deemed in that society to be moral; but knowledge of the rules or laws is, Locke firmly believed, insufficient to make people follow those laws. Good and evil are for him "nothing but Pleasure or Pain, or that which occasions, or procures Pleasure or Pain to us" (2.28.5). *Moral* good and evil combine the reference to a rule with good or evil (i.e. pleasure or pain) in the form of rewards or punishments. Those rewards or punishments may be as severe as those to be meted out to all of us at the resurrection, or as subtle as pride and shame in the educational or family context. In between come the range of sanctions and recognitions woven into the customs, practices and laws of a political society.

We learn something more about Locke's view of human nature by his insistence on the need for rewards and punishments. It would be, he says, "utterly in vain, to suppose a Rule set to the free Actions of Man, without annexing to it some Enforcement of Good or Evil, to determine his Will" (2.28.6). There are three sorts of laws to which actions are referred to determine their moral rectitude or obliquity: divine law, civil law, and the law of opinion or reputation (2.28.7). The enforcers for the third of these laws are the praise or blame of society. The force of custom, peer pressure, is effective for conforming behaviour. The enforcers for civil law are the punishments prescribed by those laws and by one's society for breaking them. The divine law has the strongest and most lasting enforcement: Locke reminds us often of that Great Day when all shall receive according to our due. Without the power to enforce a law, no law-maker can be effective. In the case of the divine law, the incentive to obey is not all negative: there is "nothing, that so directly, and visibly secures, and advances the general Good of Mankind in this World, as Obedience to the Laws, he has set them" (2.28.11).

A look at the history of mankind reveals, Locke affirms, that most men "govern themselves chiefly, if not solely" by the "Law of Fashion", a reminder again that commendation and disgrace are "strong Motives on Men" (2.28.12). Locke urges the tutor to employ these ways of determining the will of the child. We have noticed how Locke recognized the need to work with the nature of the child, allowing for natural differences. He even envisaged cases of children who may be recalcitrant, instances where it is very difficult to help a child develop into a virtuous person. All the shrewd advice and detailed observation on children in *Some Thoughts concerning Education* are directed toward socializing the child, toward bringing him to rationality by conforming his activities to the customs of his (Locke's) society and to the divine law.

We must ask, Does that emphasis on habituating the child to virtue and good manners, the emphasis on conforming to accepted modes of behaviour, allow room for individual initiative and decision? A too controlled conditioning at an early age may harm or even prevent the growth of moral man into a responsible person. Locke clearly believed that the answer to my question was 'no': a free, responsible person can only be one who is rule-following, where the rules are the measure of rationality and virtue. Support for answering this question in the affirmative also comes from the understanding Locke shows of children, and from his insistence that children should be dealt with in rational ways. By treating them rationally, giving them reasons for what we ask them to do, we are in effect addressing them as persons, at least as potential persons. Thus, the move from moral man to person is not made only by conforming the child's behaviour to rules of virtue, it is also aided by our viewing them as persons. Their inherent natural differences help prevent too much uniformity.

ACTION WORDS AS SOCIAL ARCHETYPES

Nevertheless, the potential tensions between individual freedom and social pressures are found in a number of places in Locke's writings. One interesting area where these tensions can be found is in his account of human action. Our ideas or concepts, as our words, for characterizing actions come under the heading of 'mixed modes'. A mixed mode in Locke's usage is a word or idea which functions as a name for certain features of an action, features which we, the language users and the actors, select as worthy of a separate designation. Naming is always for Locke (and for most, but not all, people at that time) conventional, even the names for objects and events in the physical world. The difference between the names for actions and those for objects and events is that the latter must refer to objects and events that can be found and described. Our description of the properties of gold must fit that metal, the good scientist gives correct descriptions of phenomena. Our names for actions must also, of course, convey an accurate understanding of the features of the actions, but we have words and concepts for actions which may never occur, only occur occasionally or only in some societies, or which mark ideals. When we do pick out features of actions and give them a name, the name is in a sense prior to the action. One way in which it is prior is in its role as what Locke calls an 'archetype', a standard or measure which an action must fit to warrant that name. Mixed modes are "assemblages of *Ideas* put together at the pleasure of the Mind, pursuing its own ends of Discourse, and suited to its own Notions" (*Essay*, 3.9.7). This reversal of the name-thing relation as it holds in science was one of the motives behind Locke's confident (over-confident, as it turned out) claim that morality could be demonstrated. Another way in which action names are prior to the action is that the action is not possible without the name and concept.

Some examples will help illustrate this apparent paradox about the action-creating role of the names or ideas (complex ideas, in Locke's terminology) of kinds of action.

> Thus, though the killing of an old Man be as fit in Nature to be united into one complex *Idea*, as the killing a Man's Father; yet, there being no name standing precisely for the one, as there is the name of *Parricide* to mark the other, it is not taken for a particular complex *Idea*, nor a distinct Species of Actions, from that of killing a young Man, or any other Man. (2.22.4)

In this example, the killing of an old man can occur, but we do not single it out as a particular kind of killing, in the way in which 'parricide' does.

> Thus we see, that killing a Man with a Sword, or a Hatchet, are looked on as a no distinct species of Action: But if the Point of the Sword first enter the Body, it passes for a distinct *Species*, where it has a distinct *Name*, as in *England*, in whose Language it is called *Stabbing*: But in another Country, where it has not happened to be specified under a peculiar *Name*, it passes not for a distinct *Species*. (3.5.11)

In a country lacking the word or concept 'stabbing', you cannot stab a man to death, although of course you *can* kill a man by first pushing the point of a sword or dagger into his body. Action words call attention to certain ways of acting, introducing into the society those kinds of actions. There are many other examples of such words in Locke's *Essay*: e.g. sham, wheedle, banter, justice, gratitude.

What these examples show is that *an action* under a definite description is in an important way dependent upon that description and its name or idea. Another feature of actions which shows their dependence upon language and thought is the psychological component. A human action, especially an action which falls under a rule or law, consists of more than just physical movements. What action words signify, words such as 'murder' or 'sacrilege' for example, "can never be known from Things themselves", from the outward motion and behaviour.

> There be many of the parts of those complex *Ideas*, which are not visible in the Action it self, the intention of the Mind, or the Relation of holy Things, which make a part of *Murther*, or

Sacrilege, have no necessary connexion with the outward and visible Action of him that commits either: and the pulling the Trigger of the Gun, with which the Murther is committed, and is all the Action, that, perhaps, is visible, has no natural connexion with those other *Ideas*, that make up the complex one, named *Murther*. (3.9.7)

The features constituting acts of murder or sacrilege are put together by men. One of the early drafts of the *Essay* makes this point even more strikingly:

A mans holding a gun in his hand & pulling downe the triger may be either Rebellion Parricide. Murther. Homicide. Duty. Justice. Valor. or recreation. & be thus variously diversified when all the circumtances put together are compard to a rule, though the simple action of holding the gun & pulling the triger may be exactly the same.[1]

To know which description fits the action we must know not only the intentions and motives of the person, but also the customs and conventions of his society. Words and concepts capture those conventions. Without the relevant knowledge, and without the proper concepts, a person cannot be said to have acted under any of those descriptions, even though the outward performance may fit some of them.

In this way, a person is a captive of his society, of its thought and language. The power of descriptive, scientific language lies in its serving us in our efforts to characterize and understand nature. Without a language sufficiently rich and flexible, science will be handicapped, or will be driven to use diagrams and symbolic devices. The power of moral discourse does not lie in its descriptive quality but in the distinctions and standards it enables us to construct. Moral language, and action words in general, have, on Locke's view, greater freedom from the events to which they refer. A society in which the moral language was not exemplified by human actions and relations would not be a useful language, although such a language would not suffer (and the society would surely benefit) were there never any instances of the actions selected by that language as negative, as evil or criminal. An utopia would be one instance of such a situation.

Moral education results in the acquisition of specific habits and also the acquisition of a moral vocabulary, with the ideas that accompany those words. What Locke's person has, which his moral man is struggling to acquire, is an understanding of the language and concepts which characterize (and sanction or abjure) responsible actions. My cognitive array of concepts helps me to appropriate my actions, to accept them under the descriptions identified by the language of my society. The language and concepts which I absorb in growing up help me fit my intentions and motives to the habits and outward performances I have acquired. This account of the action-generating nature of the language and thought of my society strengthens Locke's dramatic distinction between man and person. The parallels between the appropriating consciousness and the action-creating role of moral language (of mixed modes) are significant. Both identify and appropriate, forcing us to accept responsibility for what we do. Our moral language selects the features of human action which are important for self and society. Language and consciousness highlight the forensic aspect of the term 'person'.

SOCIAL GROUPINGS

The interplay in moral education between the socializing features of habituation to virtue, the acquisition of a vocabulary for action, and the appropriation of these as *mine*: this interplay of socializing and individualizing forces reflects a common theme in Locke's more general account of society. Every society has specific goals and purposes which mark it off from others. We move in and out of various kinds of organizations during our lives, but we are always members of some group, of some society. There is no suggestion with Locke that the individual is ever alone or asocial. "God having made Man such a Creature, that, in his own Judgment, it was not good for him to be alone, put him under strong Obligations of Necessity, Convenience, and Inclination to drive him into *Society*, as well fitted him with Understanding and Language to continue and enjoy it"(TII:77). His political theory is not grounded on a pre-political condition of single individuals struggling for survival. Locke's state of nature (that oft-used concept for starting accounts of political society) is a social and moral state, even though the responsibility for administering the law of nature falls to each individual alone. The concept of the state of nature for Locke is much broader in scope than it was for other writers at that time, since for him it encompasses any condition which does not contain the very specific goal of political society: the protection of life, liberty and possessions. Society takes many forms: family, tribe, club, religious and civil groups.[2] Locke's individual is always in a social context. Indeed, without the context of a nurturing society to care for and treat children as persons, an essential condition for making those transitions from man to moral man and then to person would be lacking.

It might be tempting to think of the transition from a state of nature to a civil society as resembling in some ways the individual's move from man or moral man to person. There *are* some similarities, but they do not include a move from social immaturity to social and moral maturity. Locke does conceive of societies as being kinds of individuals. The body politic, the community's judgement and actions, the will of the people, the corporate person: these are themes found in political writings from Hobbes to Rousseau and beyond. This way of thinking and talking about political society reveals some basic views Locke held. The notion of the state as having duties and obligations might be viewed as analogous to Locke's person: a fully self-conscious condition, constructed on a rational basis (e.g. with a social contract and the law of nature), where the civil society accepts its actions as its responsibility. It is this concept of a society acting as one body which, we will see shortly, adds another important socializing factor to the growth of persons. The analogy between the human person and the corporate person can, however, be pushed too far. Nevertheless, Locke's civil society *is* one which is governed by the laws of nature, and it *is* a society in which moral responsibility is paramount. The mechanics of government are not subjugated to moral demands, but they may not violate the single goal of protecting the person, as Locke defined him.

If we fail to note the very special nature of Locke's 'person,' we may not appreciate the significance that what civil society is designed to do is to provide security for *that* person, not just for individuals. The civil society Locke envisaged contains individuals in various states of progression from man to person.

That society is a dynamic one where the education of children occurs and various associations are formed. The account of education Locke gives concerns for the most part boys. This fact was not only a consequence of his book being the outgrowth of requests Locke had from the Clarkes on how to raise their son. The fact that Locke speaks mainly of boys and men reflects the attitudes and the conventions of his time. The mention of a contract for the conjugal society, a contract which clearly gives the woman of a marriage an equal right to separate once the children have reached the age of reason, does suggest more 'modern' views.

> The *Power of the Husband* being so far from that of an absolute Monarch, that the *Wife* has, in many cases, a Liberty to *separate* from him; where natural Right, or their Contract allows it, whether that Contract be made by themselves in the state of Nature, or by the Customs or Laws of the Countrey they live in; and the Children upon such Separation fall to the Father or Mother's Lot, as such Contract does determine. (TII:82)

On the other hand, without a full education, and without career opportunities for women (and without limited numbers of children), one may well question the possibility (certainly, the wisdom) of a wife's acting on or invoking that clause in the contract. Nevertheless, we need to use some caution in drawing any conclusion which suggests that the citizens of Locke's civil society are only male, or that the special sense of his term 'person' was meant to apply only to men.

Locke does not address the question of the total reference of the term 'person'. Since his explication of that term does not contain any conditions about pertaining only to men, or only to free men, and since there are no conceptual constraints tending in that direction, we can note our reservations about the role of women in his exposition and then extend our understanding of his account of the person and society to whomever we include under our notion. Whichever system we work with – Locke's or our own – we need to appreciate the interconnecting roles played by social forces and individual human nature in the development and protection of the person.

THE HUMANITY OF THE LAW OF NATURE

Locke names a variety of social groupings, he pays some detailed attention to the family (its structure and relations), and he discusses the Church as a society, but the society given most attention is civil or political society. It is this latter in which the others exist; it is also this society which provides the macrostructure for the order and security required by the person to lead a moral life.

Locke rejected two notions of the legitimate origins of political society: first, Robert Filmer's notion (against which he wrote extensively in the first of the *Two Treatises*) of the right of the father and the inheritance of political power via Adam (and hence ultimately from God), and second, the notion (probably that of Hobbes) that "all Government in the World is the product only of Force and Violence, and that Men live together by no other Rules but that of Beasts, where the strongest carries it."[3] Locke defines political power as "*a Right* of making Laws with Penalties of Death, and consequently all less Penalties, for the Regulating and Preserving of Property, and of employing the force of the Community, in the Execution of such Laws, and in the defence of the Common-wealth from Foreign Injury, and all this only for the Publick Good"(§3).

One phrase in this definition of political power is especially important for our later discussion, "the force of the Community". That phrase identifies one of the main characteristics which differentiate the life of the individual in the civil society and life in the state of nature. Civil society is an artificial condition. Our *natural* state, the "State all Men are naturally in" is one of "perfect Freedom to order their Actions, and dispose of their Possessions, and Persons as they think fit" (§4). Freedom has very precise boundaries, however. In our natural state our actions must be "within the bounds of the Law of Nature". We do not have to ask permission of others for what we do, nor do our actions depend upon the "Will of any other Man". It is the independence from others – not from laws of nature regulating our actions – which marks the difference between the natural and the artificial (i.e. civil) condition. But even that independence has certain bounds. In civil society, it is the force of the community which enforces laws. In the state of nature, it is the power and right of each man which keeps actions conforming to the law of nature.

Perhaps the strongest, the most awesome force controlling behaviour derives from a doctrine which Locke defended (though he twice admits it is a "strange doctrine"), that in the state of nature each man is the "Executioner of the Law of Nature" (§8,13). We are "Creatures of the same species and rank", born to "all the same advantages of Nature, and the use of the same faculties" (§4). Locke remarks that Hooker (the author of *The Lawes of Ecclesiastical Polity*, 1647) argues that the natural equality of men was the foundation for the obligation "to mutual Love amongst Men", on which Hooker built justice and charity. The law of nature is in this context identified as reason, and it is said to teach "that being all equal and independent, no one ought to harm another in his Life, Health, Liberty, or Possessions" (§6). Every individual has the power and the right to legislate in terms of the law of nature and the power and the right to enforce that law. It is *because* we are all equal in the state of nature (all adults, that is) that one man can acquire a power over another, the power of enforcing the law of nature. Locke does not say what the content of that law is, but the consequence of violating it was clear in his mind. God has set "*reason* and common Equity" as the standard and measure of "the actions of Men". That much we are told the law of nature says or does (§8). When an individual transgresses that law, that individual "declares himself to live by another Rule" than the rule of reason. Locke opens this passage on punishment by saying that the 'criminal' should receive retribution only "so far as calm reason and conscience dictates, what is proportionate to his Transgression". Reparation and restraint are the goals of punishment. But as Locke continues, he warms to his subject, like a preacher in his pulpit. It is not by chance that he uses the language of transgression, repentance and trespass. The transgressor is not portrayed as breaking some minor rule or law: he "becomes dangerous to Mankind"; he has "trespassed against the whole Species, and the Peace and Safety" of the species. One wonders what example Locke has in mind. Surely, no minor crime. "A crime against mankind" is strong language. The crime of violating the law of nature and *thereby* "varying from the right Rule of reason" makes that man *degenerate*: he has declared by his action that he has "quit the Principles of Human Nature" (§10). Not only do all men in the state of nature have the right to restraint such individuals: they can *destroy* them as "things noxious" (§8). The religious tone continues: we may "bring such evil on any one, who hath transgressed that Law, as may make him repent the doing of it". Each man is the *"Executioner of the Law of Nature"*.

Section 11 does identify a crime which may seem to fit Locke's strong language: murder. Every man in the state of nature has the power and the right to kill such a man. Locke refers to the "unjust Violence and Slaughter" such a man has committed. *That* man has declared war against all mankind. Therefore, such a man (it may be significant that he does not use the word 'person') may be "destroyed as a *Lyon* or a *Tyger*, one of those wild Savage Beasts". The crime of Cain against his brother turns out to be what was on Locke's mind.

Locke opened this discussion of punishment by remarking that the power one man has over another in these situations is not an absolute or arbitrary one. He warns against excess: we should not treat the criminal in "passionate heats or [with] boundless extravagancy" of will (§8). The passion and heat of Locke's language is justified, he obviously thinks, because of the enormity of the transgression against mankind which murder was for him. Was murder the only instance of such a crime? In chapter III, "Of the State of War", Locke cites two other examples in which we have a right to exact harsh punishment. A state of war is "a State of Enmity and Destruction", but that state can exist between any two men. Declaring "by Word or Action", with a "sedate setled Design" upon another's life (not a passionate and hasty one) puts those men in a state of war. Such a declaration exposes my life to that other man, and to any others who come to his defence. Once again Locke uses the analogy with animals, declaring that "one may destroy a Man who makes War upon him . . . for the same Reason, that he may kill a *Wolf* or a *Lyon*" (§16). That reason is the fact that such a man is no longer under the ties of "the Common Law of Reason", he acts only with force and violence. Thus, any men who threaten another "may be treated as Beasts of Prey, those dangerous and noxious Creatures, that will be sure to destroy him, whenever he falls into their Power".

Falling into the power of another, especially if that be the absolute power of another, is apparently a fear Locke had (if not for himself, at least for others). Any man who even attempts to get another into such absolute power (he does not identify what forms such power might take) does "thereby *put himself into a State of War* with him" (§17). Such a man will, Locke assures us, "use me as he pleased when he got me there, and destroy me too when he had a fancy to it". There is a generalization used here about human nature: "no body can desire to *have me in his Absolute Power*, unless it be to compel me by force to that, which is against the Right of my Freedom, *i.e.*, make me a Slave" (§17). Reason tells me to look on any person who seeks to get power over me as a threat to my preservation. If someone in the state of nature takes away another's freedom, that person must *necessarily* "be supposed to have a design to take away every thing else". Getting me into his power would be instanced by a thief, who uses force to take my money (§18). Let his pretence be what it will, I "have no reason to suppose" that he would not also take away my liberty. Thus, Locke intones, "This makes it Lawful for a Man to *kill a Thief*".

Locke coupled with these harsh views on punishment the added right of reparation. Here again, he does not fill in the details of the crime he has in mind. It is a bit difficult to think what reparation could be made to the injured party (e.g. the relatives) in the case of murder. It may in this case be lesser crimes that he has in mind, for the qualifying clause speaks of recovering from the "Offender, so much as may make satisfaction for the harm he has" inflicted (§10). In a civil society, the magistrate may, if it is not incompatible with the public good, "*remit* the punishment of Criminal Offences by his own Authority", but the magistrate "cannot *remit* the satisfaction due to any private Man, for the damage he has received" (§11). By the right of *self-preservation*, "the damnified Person has this Power of appropriating to himself, the Goods or Services of the Offender". Not just goods, but services! By two other rights declared by Locke – the right all men have of *preserving all Mankind*, and the right of "doing all reasonable things" – every man in the state of nature "has a Power to kill a Murderer". Lesser transgressions of the law of nature require lesser penalties. "Each Transgression may be *punished* to that *degree*, and with so much *Severity* as will suffice to make it an ill bargain to the Offender, give him cause to repent, and terrifie others from doing the like" (§12).

Locke entertains the objection to his doctrine that every man in the state of nature has the executive power of the law of nature, that "it is unreasonable for Men to be Judges in their own Cases, that Self-love will make Men partial to themselves and their Friends" (§13). If not partial, then ill nature, passion or revenge may cause them to be excessive in punishing. In answering this objection, Locke admits that *"Civil Government* is the proper Remedy for the Inconveniences of the State of Nature." But he reminds us that absolute monarchs are also men, and hence susceptible to these same biases and excesses. Where the civil society is of that form, of an absolute monarchy, it is much better to be in the state of nature, "wherein Men are not bound to submit to the unjust will of another" (§13). Should a man, in his role of executioner of the law of nature, judge "amiss in his own, or in any other Case, he is answerable for it to the rest of Mankind". Just what form that answering to the rest of mankind would take, Locke leaves unspecified. That other phrase, "the force of the community", comes to mind, suggesting again the reliance Locke assumes on the group, on group pressure. Individual actions will be judged, both in the state of nature and in Locke's society, by the community, the community of citizens in the latter case, the community of mankind in the former.

The independence and natural liberty in the state of nature is, Locke tells us in chapter IV of the *Second Treatise*, "to be free from any Superior Power on Earth, and not to be under the Will or Legislative Authority of Man" (§22). But the notion that man in that state has "only the Law of nature for his Rule" gets rather severely qualified by the time Locke completes his portrayal of each man as the executioner of that law. So long as our actions conform to that law, we are independent of the wills of others. Just as soon as we begin to depart from what Locke assures us the law of nature or of reason prescribes, we come under the will of another, albeit the power and right of the other stems, as Locke stresses, from the law of nature itself. That law in these passages is viewed as defining what it is to be human, so any departure from its prescriptions, even such a departure as attempted robbery, places that man outside humanity. The strong religious fervour and language with which this doctrine is presented indicates the nature of the socializing force of the law of nature. Various rights are invoked by Locke: the right of doing all reasonable things, the right of preserving all mankind, and (much more specifically and manageably) the right of self-preservation.

THE POWER OF THE COMMUNITY

The dictum "the truth shall set you free" echoes throughout Locke's discussion in *Two Treatises*. The form this dictum takes in his writing is about knowledge: the law of nature makes us free, but only after we know what that law says. We are capable of knowing the law when we are mature, when we reach the age of reason. Knowledge of that law informs us how our actions can stay within its prescriptions (§59). Some individuals are incapable of acquiring this knowledge: children before the age of reason, 'lunaticks', 'ideots', and 'innocents' never can, and some madmen can only acquire that knowledge once they recover (§60). Such individuals must remain under the "Tuition and Government of others". To assume that any individual has this important knowledge of the law of nature before he has in fact acquired it is dangerous, especially if we turn such an individual "loose to an unrestrain'd Liberty, before he has Reason to guide him"; it is "to thrust him out amongst Brutes, and abandon him to a state as wretched, and as much beneath that of a Man, as theirs" (§63).

The buffer between man and brutes is the law of nature, which is a law of reason. Our faculty of reason is fitted to discover what that law says, what its measures and standards of conduct are. We rise above the beasts only because of that faculty and what it is able to discover about the nature and bounds of *human* action. It is through this law of nature, reason and humanity, that each one of us makes with "all the rest of *Mankind . . . one Community*, [makes] up one Society distinct from all other Creatures" (§128). The precariousness of the line between men and brutes was a constant worry for Locke not that he believed a great many men would violate the law of nature and cross that line, but that we might not attend to what that law says carefully enough, that parents might guide their children imperfectly and, in the state of nature particularly, that the few corrupt, vicious, degenerate men would pose a threat to the rest. Were it not for this latter type of individuals, there would be "no necessity that Men should separate from this great and natural Community" of mankind (§128). In leaving the community of mankind in order to form smaller associations of civil societies, natural man gives up the power of preserving himself and mankind, giving that power to the civil society, "to be regulated by Laws made by the Society" (§129). In the same way, the move into civil society requires each of us to give up our right to punish those degenerate violators of the law of nature, and locate that power and right in a civil authority. In leaving the great community of mankind by joining a civil society, we do not of course cease to be men, or even cease to be members of mankind. The *community* of mankind has been replaced by a series of separate civil communities. The laws of the community of mankind also carry over to, and still serve as guides for, the civil community. The end of government in civil society is "the good of Mankind" (§229).

In the state of nature, each man's actions and judgements (especially his judgements on punishments for criminals) are answerable to the rest of mankind. In civil society, we are answerable to the whole community. The state of nature is more a condition than any sort of organized community: any condition not covered by a very specific agreement, the "agreeing together mutually to enter into one Community, and make one Body Politick" (§14). More specifically, "Those who are united into one Body, and have a common establish'd Law and Judicature to appeal to, with Authority to decide Controversies between them, and punish Offenders, *are in Civil Society* one with another" (§87). The natural power men have in the state of nature (in the community of mankind) is resigned "into the hands of the Community" in civil society. The phrase "hands of society" is found in section 131. The executive power each has in the state of nature over the law of nature is given to 'the publick'. Other phrases catch this same notion of the unity and oneness of civil society. The *society* is authorized to take over my natural powers (§89). Any controversies between a member of that society and someone outside that society "are managed by the publick" (§145). Thus, "the whole Community is one Body in the State of Nature, in respect of all other States or Persons out of its Community" (§145). That is, since the community of the civil society does not form by agreement a single body with other outside groups, the state of nature community (mankind) applies in such controversies; but instead of the relation being between one individual and another, the total community of the civil society acts as one body in relation to the challenge from outside. Individuals who have legislative or executive power in civil society become public persons "vested with the Power of the Law" and are "to be consider'd as the Image, Phantom, or Representative of the Commonwealth, acted by the will of the Society" (§151). The members of that society owe obedience only to "the publick Will of the Society". Political society "act[s] as one Body" (§211), its members are "united, and combined together into one coherent living Body" (§212). The organic analogy is even extended to talk of the legislative authority as "*the Soul that gives Form, Life, and Unity* to the Commonwealth" (§212).

When any controversy arises within a civil society, e.g. between "a Prince and some of the People", where the law is not explicit, the "proper *Umpire*, in such a Case, should be the Body of the *People*" (§242). How does this public, corporate and metaphorical body act, how do we identify *its* will and judgement? Locke's answer is that "the *Majority* have a Right to act and conclude the rest" (§95). It can only be the "will and determination of the *majority*" which can *be* the acts of the one body (§96).

> For that which acts any Community, being only the consent of the individuals of it, and it being necessary to that which is one body to move one way; it is necessary the Body should move that way whither the greater force carries it, which is the *consent of the majority*: or else, it is impossible it should act or continue one Body, *one Community*, which the consent of every individual that united into it, agreed that it should. . . (§96)

These sections of *Two Treatises* (§95–9) make it quite clear how Locke cashes the metaphor of 'the body politick'. The original contract forming the civil society entails our submitting to "the determination of the *majority*" (§97); the "*consent of the majority*" is "*the act of the whole*" (§98). If the majority "cannot conclude the rest, there they cannot act as one Body" (§98).

PRIVATE PROPERTY AND PUBLIC POWER

Individualism in the state of nature is circumscribed and limited by the law of nature and the community of mankind. Individualism in civil society is absorbed and transformed into the judgement of the majority. Some private persons become public persons, public acts replace private ones. These transformations are justified in Locke's opinion because they are the mechanism for achieving the goal of protection of life, liberty, and possessions (§135). One other important feature of Locke's civil society is the power which 'the people' have to dissolve an improperly functioning society and to form a new one. This power is not, it should be noted, a power held individually by each member of the civil society. It is a power of all (or perhaps only the majority) of the people: "the *Community* may be said in this respect to be *always the Supreme Power*" (§149). As long as the duly constituted legislative authority is functioning as it should, this power held by the people cannot be exercised (§157). In fact, there are passages in *Two Treatises* which suggest that this supreme power can have little effect, even when the executive or the legislative authority makes an improper use of its power even when it seeks to "enslave, or destroy them" (§168). In such circumstances, the people can *"appeal to Heaven"*. How that appeal is to be answered, how the people are to determine the judgement of heaven, Locke leaves unsaid. He is quick to reassure his reader that this right of an appeal to heaven will not often be invoked, that it does not "lay a perpetual foundation for Disorder" (§168), since it will not be used "till the Inconvenience is so great, that the Majority feel it, and are weary of it, and find a necessity to have it amended". A later passage also speaks of the slowness of people to make changes, even when conditions are bad (§223). Even *"Great mistakes* in the ruling part, many wrong and inconvenient Laws, and all the *slips* of humane frailty will be *born by the People* without mutiny or murmur" (§225). It is not, Locke assures us, "upon every little mismanagement in publick affairs" that revolutions happen, but only "a long train of Abuses, Prevarications, and Artifices" (§225).

In later passages, however, the appeal to heaven is bypassed and the power to replace a corrupt legislator with a new one devolves upon the people immediately. "Whenever the *Legislators endeavour to take away, and destroy the Property of the People*, or to reduce them to Slavery under Arbitrary Power", a state of war is in effect. The power which the people gave to the legislators has then been forfeited. The people, then, "have a Right to resume their original Liberty" and form a new legislative body (§222). Similar stipulations apply to corrupt executors or to any other representative person or group in civil society. "*The People shall be Judge*" as to when their trust has been forfeited (§240).

Locke does not concern himself with the details of how the judgement of the people is to be viewed and acted upon in those instances where the dissolution of government is justified. He was most concerned to establish the right of such action, while also reassuring his readers that he was not, by this doctrine, laying "a *ferment* for frequent *Rebellion*" (§224). He does detail a variety of ways in which a magistrate or any public person can break the trust given to him. His most serious defence of the power of the people to dissolve a government or to make internal changes comes when he discusses the trust broken over the protection of property. It is property and its protection which is *the* most fundamental reason for leaving the community of mankind for the greater security of civil society. The concept of property includes more than just goods or possessions and land. Most strikingly, because of its strangeness to our ears, it includes *persons*: "every Man has a *Property* in his own *Person*" (§27; see also §173). Labour is also property, the property of the labourer (§27). In other passages, the scope of what is to be protected in civil society covers such items as life, health, liberty, and possessions (§6), life or property (§65), property and actions (§69). Some of these lists seem to distinguish between property and, for example, life or actions, but section 123 is explicit: "the general Name, *Property*" refers to "Lives, Liberties and Estates". What all these have in common is the fact that the items on these lists are private: *my* actions, *my* life, *my* labour, *my* liberty.

Much of Locke's writing about man's natural freedom and about the individual privacy of property was in response to Robert Filmer's *Patriarcha, or The Natural Power of Kings* (1680), the book against which the first of Locke's *Two Treatises* was written. Locke saw in Filmer's defence of absolute monarchy, and the claimed descent from Adam of the divine right to rule, an advocacy of that absolute power over others which he so much abhorred. He read *Patriarcha* as providing "Chains for all Mankind" (TI:1). Filmer had talked of the authority fathers had over their children, not just those fathers who were kings. To find Filmer saying that the father of a family governs only by his own will, went against all that Locke believed about the rights of children and the concept of humanity which he took to be embodied in the law of nature. The strong language used against Filmer reveals the passion behind Locke's defence of the life, liberty and estates of all men.

> This *Fatherly Authority*, then, or *Right of Fatherhood*, in our A---'s sence is a Divine unalterable Right of Sovereignty, whereby a Father or a Prince hath an Absolute, Arbitrary, Unlimited, and Unlimitable Power, over the Lives, Liberties, and Estates of his Children and Subjects; so that he may take or alienate their Estates, sell, castrate, or use their Persons as he pleases, they being all his Slaves, and he Lord or Proprietor of every Thing, and his unbounded Will their Law. (TI:9)

In writing about property in the second of *Two Treatises*, Locke has his eye on Filmer's claim that "God gave the World to *Adam* and his Posterity in common." Instead, Locke cites the Old Testament passage (Psalms CXV, v.16), God *"has given the Earth to the Children of Men*, given it to Mankind in common" (§25). But there is a conceptual problem Locke needs to face: if each man is to have some of what has been given to all in common, if each is to acquire some private property (which the civil society is to protect), how is privacy to emerge from the common? He offers an ingenious explanation, showing not only how a man can acquire property out of what is not property (out of what is common), but showing how that is possible without an express agreement or compact (§25). While he had asserted earlier in this same treatise that men are the property of God since they are his workmanship (§6), he apparently did not feel that fact was incompatible with my person being *my* property as well.[4] *Men* are God's property, *persons* are not. Person is, as we have seen, the most perfect form of moral man, the standard of humanity. When we appropriate our actions as our own through consciousness, we are exerting effort, labouring as it were, and accepting responsibility for what we are as moral agents. In a similar way, my actions appropriate land and goods from what was common. By mixing some of my self through labouring to till the soil or collect the fruit, I make the land and the fruit mine.

> Though the Earth, and all inferior Creatures be common to all Men, yet every Man has a *Property* in his own Person. This no Body has any Right to but himself. The *Labour* of his Body, and the *Work* of his Hands, we may say, are properly his. Whatsoever then he removes out of the State that Nature hath provided, and left it in, he hath mixed his *Labour* with, and joyned to it something that is his own, and thereby makes it his *Property*. (§27)

He goes on to say that my labour has also excluded the right of others to what I have mixed my labour with: "no Man but he can have a right to what that is once joyned to, at least where there is enough, and as good left in common for others" (§27).

The last two conditions, that enough and as good is left, were important for Locke, but the basic principle, that my labour has added something to the land over and above what 'Nature' has done (thereby making my own what my labour has produced), was Locke's resolution of the conceptual problem of how "the *Property of labour* should be able to over-ballance the Community of Land" (§40).[5] The resolution speaks to "the beginning and first peopling of the great Common of the World" (§35), not to Locke's own day, nor to his own civil society model where compact and civil law specify property rights, and where those two additional conditions no longer hold. Another modification over the situation in "the first Ages of the World" was "the *Invention of Money*, and the tacit Agreement of Men to put a value on it" (§36). Money "introduced (by Consent) larger Possessions, and a Right to them". That it may not have been money alone (or even money at all) that introduced this change, is suggested by a remark Locke goes on to make, that "the desire of having more than Men needed" was what "altered the intrinsick value of things" (§37). This desire moved men from use-value (intrinsic value) to exchange-value. Locke's anthropology does not extend so far as to trace the first appearance of this desire to have more than men need, nor does he offer a psychological explanation. It is for him a given fact that men now have that desire and that money enables it to be fulfilled.

He marks the difference between the worlds of use-value and exchange-value in several ways. First, a moral difference. If a man acquired more goods than he could use before they perished, that man "offended against the common Law of Nature, and was liable to be punished" (§37); similarly for enclosing too much land and allowing some of the grass to rot on the ground. Secondly, with use-value, the different degrees of value are a direct function of labour and its results. The difference between land uncultivated and cultivated makes the difference in value of the land (§40). Locke does not develop a quantitative measure of the amount of labour expended, but he does suggest such a notion (§43). The desire to have more was met even before the invention of money through barter. By exchanging "Plumbs that would have rotted in a Week, for Nuts that would last good for his eating a whole Year, he did no injury; he wasted not the common Stock" (§46). Or, if he exchanged his nuts for a piece of metal whose colour pleased him, or some sheep for shells, he still did not injure anyone, staying well within the dictates of the law of nature. Locke draws an important conclusion at this point: *"the exceeding of the bounds of his* just *Property* not lying in the largeness of his Possession, but the perishing of any thing uselesly in it" (§46). The stage was thus set for the invention of money, "some lasting thing that Men might keep without spoiling, and that by mutual consent Men would take in exchange for the truly useful, but perishable Supports of Life" (§47). Coupled with the fact that men had different degrees of industry, money as exchange value brought a "disproportionate and unequal Possession of the Earth" (§50). By agreeing on the use of money, men have, Locke remarks, agreed on unequal possessions.

CONCLUSION

Two human processes are described in Locke's writings. The one is the process from childhood to personhood. The child is depicted in the family setting, with a moral tutor and a tutor for instruction (usually, these tutors are a single person, if not the father himself). Tutor and parents work with the child to socialize

him, to enable him to acquire virtuous habits. The language the
child learns, with its mixed-mode words signalling virtue, picking
out bodily movements as actions, reinforces these efforts of tutor
and parents. The goal is to guide the child to the age of reason
and to personhood. The second process is the movement of the
adult from the community of mankind to the community of a
political society. Whether Locke thought he was describing an
actual historical condition in employing the notion of a state of
nature, or whether he used that notion as a convenient expository
device, it does reveal an important part of his thinking about
human nature. We are always under the jurisdiction of the law of
nature, just because it prescribes the qualities of being human.
Even when we belong to a civil polity, the laws of that community
must not clash with the law of nature. Thus, we always belong to
the great community of mankind, unless we are so foolish as to
violate its prescriptions and fall from grace, slip down the scale of
being into the ranks of the beasts.

Man starts by belonging to the community of mankind where
the earth and its contents were given by God to all men. But just
as my actions must consciously be appropriated by me so that I
can become a responsible person, so in using the land, in
gathering fruit and game, I appropriate part of the common,
making that part my property. We end by dividing up the
common. In the state of nature, the rights and duties prescribed
by the law of nature devolve upon each individual separately,
although the judgement of mankind waits in the wings to assess
our individual acts. The move into a civil society is a move from
individualism to corporatism. Even those persons who perform
official duties in the civil society do so as *public* persons, not as
private individuals. This corporatism of the body politic, of the
will of the community, of the living organism which is the total
society, is Locke's way of protecting that aspect of individualism
which is most important for him: the person and the extension of
the person, all his property (life, health, labour, estates, and
possessions). The socialization of the individual is the process
whereby the individual becomes a person, adaptable to living
with others and accepting the judgement of the group, capable
when pressed too far of invoking the law of nature in order to
correct social evils, but always having the legitimate title to what
his industry and labour have procured.

NOTES

1   *Draft A of Locke's Essay concerning Human Understanding*, Transcribed by Peter H. Nidditch (1980), §23, p. 85. Also in *An Early Draft of Locke's Essay*, edited by R.I. Aaron and Jocelyn Gibb (1936), p. 35.
2   CF. *A Letter concerning Toleration*, in *Works*, (1823 edn) vol. VI, p. 13, where Locke lists other sorts of societies: "philosophers for learning, of merchants for commerce, or of men of leisure for mutual conversation and discussion".
3   §1. For the rest of this chapter, unless otherwise noted, reference to *Two Treatises* are all to the second of the two, indicating the sections only.
4   For an analysis of the workmanship model, see James Tully's *A Discourse on Property* (1980). The index entry under "workmanship" gives many references to his discussion.
5   See also §44:

> From all which it is evident, that though the things of Nature are given in common, yet Man (by being Master of himself, and *Proprietor of his own Person*, and the Actions or *Labour* of it) had still in himself *the great Foundation of Property*; and that which made up the great part of what he applyed to the Support or Comfort of his being, when Invention and Arts had improved the conveniencies of Life, was perfectly his own, and did not belong in common to others.

4

The Rationality of Religion

There is a remark often quoted from the preface "To the Reader" of *A Letter concerning Toleration* which, while not by Locke, can be seen as catching something of his view: "*Absolute Liberty, just and true liberty, equal and impartial liberty, is the thing that we stand in need of*".[1] As we have seen, the move into a civil society entailed for him the loss of some of the liberty each man had in the state of nature. It is true that men exchanged for that liberty the peace and security of a well-ordered society. Furthermore, civil society with its legal safeguards and with the organic structure of a body politic, does provide, Locke believed, an encouraging setting for the development of moral man and person. At the same time, we need to recognize that while in the state of nature man was (as Locke remarked in a very early tract on government) "naturally owner of an entire liberty, and so much master of himself as to owe no subjection to any other but God", in the civil society that liberty had to be entrusted to the magistrate "with as full a power over all his actions as he himself hath".[2]

CIVIL AND RELIGIOUS AUTHORITY

In this early writing on government, Locke did not decide which was the better form of government, monarchy or a commonwealth (although, writing at that time after the Restoration, he was obviously relieved to have a king returned to the throne), mainly because of his belief that men do not "enjoy any greater share of . . . freedom in a pure commonwealth . . .

than in an absolute monarchy" (*ibid.*). His reason is that "the same arbitrary power" is in "the assembly (which acts like one person) as in a monarch" (*ibid.*). All that any man can do is to persuade the majority or the monarch. If "the supreme authority and power of making laws be conferred on the magistrate by the consent of the people", it follows that "all his commands are but their own votes, and his edicts their own injunctions made by proxy which by mutal contract they are bound to obey" (*ibid.*, p. 126). The magistrate, whether in a monarchy or in a commonwealth, "concentrates in his person the authority and natural right of every individual by a general contract" (*ibid.*, p. 231).

There were, however, two clearly related areas which were exempt from the magistrates' control and jurisdiction: morality and religion.[3] The vague notion of the law of reason or nature was one source for morality, the Bible was the source for specific moral rules and the doctrines necessary for religious belief. Even where people were inclined to agree with Locke on the separation of items of civil interest and those concerned with morality and religion, there was not always agreement on the demarcation line. The separation is not clean. There are aspects of religious practices which have or can have an effect outside the religious society, practices that impinge upon public and civil affairs. The civil society and the magistrate do have an obligation to construct laws consistent with the moral law and conducive to encouraging morality. Thus in both these areas of morality and religion there are aspects which cannot be entirely separated from civil interests. There was some agreement on what constituted "indifferent things", the phrase then in use, that is, things indifferent to the salvation of souls and to religious belief, but there was disagreement as to whether the civil magistrate had any jurisdiction over such indifferent things as the time and place of worship, public prayers, acts of thanksgiving, the appearance, posture, and dress in religious services (*Two Tracts*, p. 215).

Locke tried to identify the area of civil interest in his *A Letter concerning Toleration*: "life, liberty, health, and indolency of body; and the possession of outward things, such as money, land, houses, furniture, and the like" (p. 10). He wrote this *Letter* to delimit the magistrate's jurisdiction to these areas only, excluding him from any activity relating to the salvation of souls. The magistrate has no better knowledge of the way to heaven than any private person (p. 26). Distinguishing between the "outward form and rites of worship" and "the doctrines and articles of faith", the *Letter* says unequivocally that "the magistrate has no power to enforce by law, either in his own church, or much less in another, the use of any rites or ceremonies whatsoever in the worship of God" (p. 29). Earlier, in *Two Tracts*, he was not so emphatic in his exclusion of the magistrate from these areas. In fact, he argued there that "God left many indifferent things untrammelled by his laws and handed them to his deputy the magistrate" (p. 223). All indifferent actions (i.e. those that are neither moral or immoral, and those not related to the salvation of souls) "must and ought in all societies be resigned freely into the hands of the magistrate" (p. 129).

In *Two Tracts*, Locke gives a variety of reasons for his defence of this claim. Most of the activities that count as indifferent were tied in with the customs of each society, customs that mark the way of life of that people. It would have been impossible, as well as unwise, for the divine law even to attempt uniformity, to lay down standards for all societies (p. 216). He also observes that danger lies in claiming that the magistrate should have no say in indifferent matters, for people would then take advantage, declaring whatever suited their interests as indifferent.

> Let the people (whose ears are always open to complaints against their governors, who greedily swallow all pleas for liberty) but once hear that the magistrate hath no authority to enjoin things indifferent in matters of religion, they will all of an instant be converts, conscience and religion shall presently mingle itself with all their actions and be spread over their whole lives to protect them from the reach of the magistrate, and they will quickly find the large extent of *inordine ad spiritualia*. (p. 154)

Intolerance also lies this way (p. 159).

This debate over the precise bounds between civil and religious matters, especially over the particular issues to which Locke was responding, was a local and time-bound controversy. Whatever his reasons for not publishing these early tracts, they are still informative in showing Locke's careful attention to details, to reasons and arguments. Those tracts also show that Locke had the notion early of a political society being like a person, with its attendant tensions between the individual and the corporate person. Just what the extent would be of the magistrate's or the corporate community's absorbing the customs and practices of men under the heading of "indifferent things", is not entirely clear especially in his later *Two Treatises*. What we can say about *Two Tracts* is that they reveal a strong concern by Locke for the role of religion in society. He appreciated the importance of local customs and forms of life, local variations even in religious practices. He was also sensitive to the need for toleration of idiosyncratic habits and modes of behaviour, toleration on the part of the magistrate and of each individual. The assigning of matters indifferent to the civil authority should not be used as a cover for intolerance. The distinction between matters civil and matters religious becomes important so that "none may impose either upon himself or others, by the pretences of loyalty and obedience to the prince" (*Letter*, p. 9). The preface "To the Reader" of the *Letter concerning Toleration* laments the partial and inadequate attempts made in England to expand and establish religious toleration, e.g., "declarations of indulgence" and "acts of comprehension" (p. 3). What Locke sets out to do in this work is to examine the question of toleration rationally by explicating some of the basic concepts: religion, church and faith.

True religion is, he declares, "not instituted in order to the erecting an eternal pomp, nor to the obtaining of ecclesiastical dominion, nor in the exercising of compulsive force; but to the regulating of men's lives according to the rules of virtue and piety" (p. 6). Moreover, "all the life and power of true religion consists in the inward and full persuasion of the mind, and faith is not faith without believing" (pp. 10–11). A church is defined as a voluntary society of men, "joining themselves together of their own accord, in order to the public worshipping of God" (p. 13). Locke sees no need for a church to have "a bishop, or presbyter, with ruling authority derived from the very apostles" (p. 14). He finds no support in the Bible for such an apparatus; the concept of a church does not include anything other than the features he specifies. He is not intolerant of those churches which do include other features, but he makes a plea for toleration of his own minimalist defintion:

But since men are so solicitous about the true church, I would only

ask them here by the way, if it be not more agreeable to the church
of Christ to make the conditions of her communion consist in such
things, and such things only, as the Holy Spirit has in the holy
Scriptures declared in express words, to be necessary to
salvation?" (p. 15)

Membership in a church or religious society is voluntary, based
on belief. The only force besides persuasion that should be used
by that society on its members is expulsion. The church does not
need to keep a member who offends against the laws of the
society (p. 16). No civil injury or sanctions should be levied
against a person who has been excommunicated by a church. Nor
should any private person "prejudice another person in his civil
enjoyments, because he is of another church or religion" (p. 17).
Different churches stand in the same relation to each other: no
one has any jurisdiction over any other, "every church is
orthodox to itself; to others, erroneous, or heretical", but each
should be tolerant of the other (p. 18). In short, "Nobody
therefore . . . neither single persons, nor churches, nay, nor even
commonwealths, have any just title to invade the civil rights and
worldly goods of each other, upon pretence of religion" (p. 20).

ARTICLES OF FAITH AND SCRIPTURAL VIRTUE

Locke points to past history in his own country to remind his
readers how easy it has been for ecclesiastical authority to adapt
itself to the different whims or fancies of monarchs, changing
their decrees, their form of worship, even their articles of faith to
fit the current vogue. There are two important considerations
that he urges which have the consequence of keeping religion
separate from civil authority. One of these calls for a careful
distinction between the doctrines said to be necessary for belief
by the clergy and the doctrines required by the Bible and by
Jesus's example. These latter, as we will see, are very minimal.
The second consideration calls attention to the necessary
condition of belief for accepting any religion. A man cannot be
forced to believe, although he can and should be exhorted to do
so. Nor can a man be saved by a religion whose doctrines he does
not accept.

No way whatsoever that I shall walk in against the dictates of my conscience, will ever bring me to the mansions of the blessed. I may grow rich by an art that I take not delight in; I may be cured of some disease by remedies that I have not faith in; but I cannot be saved by a religion that I distrust, and by a worship that I abhor. (p. 28)

In discussing belief and the articles of faith in the *Letter*, Locke distinguishes between practical and speculative articles. Both consist in the knowledge of truth but the speculative articles terminate in the understanding while the practical ones "influence the will and manners" (p. 39). In this work, Locke was primarily concerned to guard against the civil authority's encroaching upon either type of article. Even a heathen who rejects both the Old and New Testaments of the Bible should not be punished "as a pernicious citizen" (p. 40); but in a later passage, Lake makes it clear that the atheist falls outside the scope of toleration (perhaps too, outside the community of mankind),[4] whether civil or religious:

Lastly, Those are not at all to be tolerated who deny the being of God. Promises, covenants, and oaths, which are the bonds of human society, can have no hold upon an atheist. The taking away of God, though but even in thought, dissolves all. (p. 47)

To discover what the articles of faith are for Locke's interpretation of the Christian religion, we must turn to his *Reasonableness of Christianity*. Just as the *Letter* rejected as unnecessary and unauthorized by the Scriptures a church apparatus, an ecclesiastical hierarchy, so Locke takes a minimalist view of the doctrines required for Christian belief. In the *Reasonableness* he indicates in the Preface that he was dissatisfied with *systems* of divinity. His method was to return to the Scriptures in order to see what was required. Consistent with his later *Paraphrases of St. Paul's Epistles* where, in the important Introduction, Locke laid down the principles to be used in reading an ancient text, he insists in the *Reasonableness* that since the New Testament is "a collection of writings, designed by God, for the instruction of the illiterate bulk of mankind", it is to be understood

in the plain direct meaning of the words and phrases: such as they

may be supposed to have had in the mouths of the speakers, who
used them according to the language of that time and country
wherein they lived; without such learned, artificial, and forced
senses of them, as are sought out, and put upon them, in most of
the systems of divinity, according to the notions that each one has
been bred up in.[5]

To understand what is required to be believed by a Christian, we
need first, Locke observes, to ask what we lost through Adam's
fall. He found two extremes among the interpretations then
current. One view said that all men are doomed to eternal
punishment because of Adam's fall, even though "millions had
never heard of [him], and no one had authorised [Adam] to
transact for him, or be his representative" (p. 4). The other
extreme was that of natural religion, which claimed that this first
view was inconsistent with the goodness and justice of God and
hence that no redemption is necessary for men. Both extremes
distort the New Testament teaching. A reading of these
Scriptures unbiassed by these interpretations shows, Locke
maintains, that "what Adam fell from . . . was the state of perfect
obedience, which is called justice in the New Testament" (p. 5).
Locke takes the reader carefully through the Scriptures in order
to show the exact, plain meaning of Adam's fall and Jesus's
redemption. The details of his exegesis need not concern us,
other than its conclusion which tells us what we need to believe.
What Locke calls "the law of faith" requires, first of all, each man
to believe what God "requires him to believe, as a condition of
the convenant he makes with him: and not to doubt of the
performance of his promises" (p. 16). More specifically, the
passage from John iii: 36 – "He that believeth on the Son, hath
eternal life" is rendered by Locke as: "believing on the Son is the
believing that Jesus was the Messiah" (p. 17). This belief entails
"giving credit to the miracles he did, and the profession he made
of himself" (*ibid.*). Believing Jesus to be the Messiah also entails
believing that he rose from the dead (p. 20).

To his minimalist interpretation of what we are required to
believe in order to be a Christian (that Jesus is the Messiah),
Locke suggested that it may be objected that that belief gives us
only "an historical, and not a justifying, or saving faith" (p. 101).
This is an objection from those systematizers whose
interpretations Locke does not find supported by the Bible. If

these people want to call the faith that goes with Locke's belief an historical one, he has no real objection, but when they deny that it is a justifying or saving one, he insists that "our Saviour and his apostles have declared it" to be precisely that (p. 102). He challenges those who raise this objection to show him "that there was any other doctrine upon their assent to which, or disbelief of it, men were pronounced believers or unbelievers; and accordingly received into the church of Christ, as members of his body" (p. 102). One other condition was required along with the belief: repentance (p. 103). He explains that repentance "does not consist in one single act of sorrow" but in obeying "the law of Christ, the remainder of our lives" (p. 105). In short, we must believe Jesus to be the Messiah and also lead a good life, the law of faith must be joined with the law of works.

Various labels are to be found in the *Reasonableness* for the law which shows us how to behave: the law of Christ, of God, of reason, of right, of nature. These labels name "the eternal and established law of right and wrong" (p. 10). Obeying this law which prescribes our moral duties is important not only for the salvation of our souls, but for the existence of government and civil society (p. 11). The duties of the law of nature arise from the constitution of man's nature (p. 112). Our reason is fitted to discover that law unassisted, but, as we have seen, Locke does not produce the rational derivation which he thought possible. Moreover, in the *Reasonableness* he admits that such a derivation is neither easy nor open to many men. The safest way to discover what the law of nature teaches is through revelation, as recorded in the Scriptures. Locke asserts confidently that all the duties of morality have been cited and used in the Scriptural account of Jesus and his apostles (p. 122). Scriptural morality should be our guide.

What we discover from a careful reading of the Scriptures is that "a man should forgive, not only his children, but his enemies, upon their repentance" (p. 133). Other more specific virtues and vices are extracted from Jesus's sermon on the mount, as narrated by Matthew and Luke. There, Jesus tells men:

> That not only murder, but causeless anger, and so much as words of contempt, were forbidden. He commands them to be reconciled and kind towards their adversaries; and that upon pain of

condemnation . . . he not only forbids actual uncleanness, but all irregular desires, upon pain of hell-fire; causeless divorces; swearing in conversation, as well as forswearing in judgment; revenge; retaliation; ostentation of charity, of devotion, and of fasting; repetitions in prayer, covetousness, worldly care, censoriousness: and on the other side commands loving our enemies, doing good to those that hate us, blessing those that curse us, praying for those that despitefully use us; patience and meekness under injuries, forgiveness, liberality, compassion. (p. 115)

FAITH AND REASON

From the specificity of lists of Christian virtue such as this one, from the constant stress in the *Reasonableness* upon the importance of good works, and from the coupling of belief in Jesus as the Messiah with the need for repentance, we can draw the conclusion that Scriptural virtue is almost of greater importance for Locke than belief. Of course, they must go together, as Locke makes abundantly clear. But we know the prominence he gave to habituating children into good behaviour: it is a prelude to the fully moral person. Did he also see acting virtuously as a prelude to religious belief? Presumably the child would be exhorted, even admonished, to believe, but how did that "inward persuasion of the mind" on which religion is based occur? The early *Essays on the Law of Nature* show how the belief in the existence of a god arises through a combination of reason and experience.[6] Locke echoes this view in the *Letter* when he writes: "It is only light and evidence that can work a change in man's opinions" (p. 12). But the belief in a supreme God, architect of the world and lawmaker, is a different sort of belief from believing Jesus to be the Messiah and having risen from the dead. The only basis for taking this latter belief to be true is if I also accept the Bible as the word of God. It was one thing for the apostles to witness the miracles performed by Jesus and then to believe he was the son of God. It is rather different for us to acquire that belief from reading about those miracles.

Locke gives ample attention in his *Essay* to the nature, role and provenance of belief and opinion. For one who, like Locke, found the extent of human knowledge limited, it was necessary to find some other basis on which man can act. Had we to rely only upon the certainty of true knowledge, man would be "perfectly at a stand" in most of the actions of life, not knowing how, or even daring, to act (*Essay*, 4.14.1). The world in which we now live is a prelude to the next world. The limitations of our knowledge, "Our short-sightedness and liableness to Error", might be, Locke conjectures, "a constant Admonition to us, to spend the days of this our Pilgrimage with Industry and Care, in the search, and following of that way, which might lead us to a State of greater Perfection" (4.14.2). Judgement is the faculty God has given us to take over where understanding and knowledge fails. In making judgements, we *presume* such and such to be the case, upon proper evidence, to be sure. Just as demonstration or the showing of certain connections leads to knowledge, so probability is the appearance of those connections (4.15.1). Another way of speaking about probability is to say it "is likeliness to be true", when we entertain a probable proposition we believe or assent to it, hold an opinion about it (§3). As we shall see later, one strong sense of 'knowledge' and 'know' for Locke is found when what we know testifies to its truth, the intuition that comes with understanding. For belief, on the other hand, what makes us believe some proposition or state of affairs, is "something extraneous to" the proposition or state of affairs. There is a difference between the *marks of knowledge* and the *marks of probability*, a difference of some importance for Locke's analysis of religious belief.

Recognition of the limitations of our knowledge, and of the tentative nature of our probable beliefs and opinions, ought to lead, Locke suggests, to a tolerance of those people holding beliefs different from ours (4.16.4). Instead of attacking the beliefs of others, we should strive to find better grounds for our own. "The necessity of believing, without Knowledge, nay, often upon very slight grounds, in this fleeting state of Action and Blindness we are in, should make us more busy and careful to inform our selves, than constrain others" (4.16.4). Probable propositions are of two sorts: those dealing with matters of fact and observation, for which human testimony can vouch, and those "which being beyond the discovery of our Senses, are not capable of any such Testimony" (4.16.5). The first sort deal with the nature of things themselves, based on constant experience from which we draw conjectures (e.g. about the insensible nature of matter) or generalizations (e.g. about like causes having like effects) (4.16.6). Other matters of fact are accepted only on the testimony of others, e.g. historians, not as a result of our own acquaintance (4.16.8). When we encounter conflicting testimonies, we can only weigh all sides and form a belief, conjecture, guess, doubt, or disbelief, as the case seems to warrant (4.16.9).

Locke gives other examples of the first sort of belief, beliefs formed on the basis of our own experience or on what we take to be good testimony of others. But he calls attention to a different type of case where the strangeness of the fact not only does not lessen our assent, but even strengthens it: the case of *miracles* (4.16.13). In a short "Discourse on Miracles" he defines a miracle as: "a sensible operation, which, being above the comprehension of the spectator, and in his opinion contrary to the established course of nature, is taken by him to be divine".[7] The phrase, "in his opinion", raises difficulties, for it seems to make miracles relative to the extent of our knowledge. By way of dealing with this difficulty, Locke remarks that we are either spectators of the event which we take to be a miracle (e.g. as Moses was with the burning bush or the rod turned to a serpent) or when we accept the historical account of such events (when we are "in the place of a spectator", spectators at second-hand). Since our judgement of what surpasses the laws of nature or goes against the ordinary course of events may vary, depending upon the extent of our experience and knowledge, what may be judged a miracle by one man may not be so judged by another. Locke also seems to allow for miracles not caused by God. What he wants to protect is our ability to be able to recognize a miracle as a sign from God, as attesting to its divine origin, as revelation. "To know that any revelation is from God, it is necessary to know that the messenger that delivers it is sent from God, and that cannot be known but by some credentials given him by God himself" ("Discourse on Miracles" p. 257).

What are the marks which inform us that some extraordinary event is in fact a miracle, that it was "wrought by God himself for the attestation of a revelation from him" (p. 259)? Locke's first answer paints a scenario of competing messengers, each claiming to bring the divine word. The true miracle will reveal a greater power than the competing conjuring trick. "The producing of serpents, blood, and frogs, by the Egyptian Sorcerers and by Moses, could not to the spectators but appear equally miraculous", but when "Moses' serpent eat up theirs", the difference was clear (p. 260). Another criterion of miracles wrought by God rather than by sorcerers is "the number, variety, and greatness of the miracle", as for example the ones used in confirming the doctrines delivered by Jesus (p. 261). These miracles all carry, Locke claims in his *Discourse*, "strong marks of an extraordinary divine power", supernatural signs (pp. 261,262).

Such signs cannot deceive, they carry an "Assurance beyond Doubt, Evidence beyond Exception", they are called "revelation" and our assent to them is faith *(Essay*, 4.16.14). A more formal definition of "faith" is given in *Essay* 4.18.2: "the Assent to any Proposition, not thus made out by the Deductions of Reason; but upon the Credit of the Proposer, as coming from GOD, in some extraordinary way of Communication". The *Discourse* describes what in the *Essay* is called *original revelation*, but Locke recognized that we only have the words of those spectators who witnessed Jesus's miracles. *Traditional revelation*, such as the Scriptures, must use words to describe what was seen and heard. Words and language have a number of limitations on Locke's account, a limitation in traditional revelation being that words cannot convey any new simple ideas, ideas which do not depend upon other ideas for their sense or meaning.

> Thus whatever Things were discovered to St. *Paul*, when he was rapp'd up into the Third Heaven; whatever new *Ideas* his Mind there received, all the description he can make to others of that Place, is only this, That there are such Things, *as Eye hath not seen, nor Ear heard, nor hath it entred into the Heart of Man to conceive*. (4.18.3)

Revelation need not be limited to the extraordinary, to things not seen, heard, or conceived. God could reveal to us the truths of Euclid. Such a revelation would, however, be superfluous since God has given us natural faculties so that we can discover and understand those truths. Where our natural faculties are able to make discovery, revelation is not needed. Moreover, there is an inherent difficulty were revelation made of truths which our natural faculties can come to know. "For the Knowledge, we have, that this *Revelation* came at first from GOD, can never be so sure, as the Knowledge we have from the clear and distinct Perception of the Agreement, or Disagreement of our own *Ideas* . . ." (4.18.4). Even were we to assent to such a revelation because it came down to us from tradition, the truth to which we would have assented will never be as certain as the knowledge we have when we study Euclid, follow his demonstrations, and come to see the connections between the ideas of line, angle, etc. Even a revelation such as that of the flood which Noah witnessed (an *original* revelation) is not as sure and certain to us as it was for Noah. I have "not so great an assurance, that *Moses* writ that Book", as I would have, had I seen him write it. Similarly, the assurance of the flood being a revelation is less for us than it was for Noah.

Suppose God does immediately reveal some truth to me which can be discovered by my natural faculties. Even then, Locke insists, "our Assurance can be no greater, than our Knowledge is, that it is a *Revelation* from GOD" (4.18.5). Moreover, we will never allow or accept as true a revealed truth which contradicts the evidence of our understanding. The evidence "of our Faculties, by which we receive such *Revelations*" can never exceed "the certainty of our intuitive Knowledge" (*ibid.*). No revelation will gain our assent to the proposition that one body can be in two places at once. This is the only example Locke gives at this point.

There is a tone about this passage, though, which suggests that Locke has in mind more than logical or conceptual truths. He warns against labelling as matter of faith any claims which go against our own clear perception. Faith "can never convince us of any Thing, that contradicts our Knowledge. Because though *Faith* be founded on the Testimony of GOD (who cannot lye) revealing any Proposition to us: yet we cannot have an assurance of the Truth of its being a divine Revelation, greater than our own Knowledge" (4.18.5). The conclusion is clear: unless we have some marks attesting that some proposition is revealed which are stronger than the evidence of our reason and understanding, we should not accept that proposition as revealed. In other words, even with immediate or original revelation, we are urged by Locke to give preference to reason, so long as the revelation does not exceed the evidence of reason and its principles. So much more, then, ought reason to be used with traditional revelation. Locke even says that in this type of revelation (such as the Scriptures contain) reason "is that only which can induce us to receive" those truths (4.18.6). Two revelations are required: one that this is a revealed truth and the other revealing the truth. Without the first revelation, "the believing, or not believing that Proposition, or Book, to be of Divine Authority, can never be Matter of *Faith*, but Matter of Reason" (*ibid.*).

These remarks apply to those truths which can be discovered by the use of our natural faculties. What about those other sort of truths, those that go beyond reason and our faculties? Examples of such truths are: "that part of the Angels rebelled against GOD, and thereby lost their first happy state", or "that the dead shall rise, and live again". With these truths, reason has nothing to do, they are "purely Matters of *Faith*" (4.18.7). Revelation also carries against the probable conjectures of reason. The explanation for this preference of revelation over reason is simply that we should give our assent to a testimony which our reason is satisfied does come from God. But here again, reason is asked to judge that that truth is in fact a revelation. Reason is also assigned the task of determining the signification of the words of the revelation. Locke returns to this central claim many times: "Whatever GOD hath revealed, is certainly true; no Doubt can be made of it. This is the proper Object of *Faith*: But whether it be a divine Revelation, or no, *Reason* must judge" (4.18.10).

THE PROBLEM OF THE CRITERION

What is lacking from Locke's account of the proper domains of reason and faith is any indication of what the marks are which, in traditional revelation, reason can take as genuine criteria of a revelation. He appears to side-step this issue. Part of the explanation for the failure to discuss this question of criteria lies in his almost obsessive concern to find room in religion for the use of reason. His *Reasonableness of Christianity* applies common sense and reason to the interpretation of Jesus's actions and words. His detailed paraphrases of St Paul give equally ordinary readings of what St Paul said and meant. "Reasonable" in part meant for Locke not extravagant, not forced, not extraordinary. Wherever he used the Bible in his discussions (and the extent to which commentary on the Bible appears in his writings is very great and in many different works),[8] his reading follows this pattern of looking for a straightforward, ordinary meaning. Religion, he remarks in the *Essay*, "should most distinguish us from Beasts, and ought most peculiarly to elevate us, as rational Creatures, above Brutes" (4.18.11). Instead, much of religion in his day was characterized by fancies and superstitions, by "extravagant Opinions and Ceremonies" contradictory to common sense. "Enthusiasm" is the name given to such extravagances. So important did this topic continue to be to Locke that he added a new chapter on this topic in the fourth edition of the *Essay*. —

Locke had a notion of some kind of relation between proof and assent. This was not a quantitative notion, but assent and assurance do have degrees. A genuine lover of truth will see to it that he not entertain "any Proposition with greater assurance than the Proofs it is built upon will warrant" (4.19.1). Demonstrations are said to have a "force", and self-evident propositions have an "irresistible light". Propositions receive their credit or authority from "the Principles and Propositions" they rest upon. Enthusiasm is taken by some men as a legitimate ground of assent, but its main fault for Locke is that it allows no room for reason and the force of arguments. The enthusiasts "set up Revelation without" reason (4.19.3). Groundless opinions which catch their fancies are, by these men, taken to be "an Illumination from the Spirit of GOD" (§6). Enthusiasm is founded "neither on Reason, nor Divine Revelation", but rises from "the Conceits of a warmed or over-weening Brain" (§7). These conceits have powerful effects on people, influencing their actions and beliefs.

> yet the Love of something extraordinary, the Ease and Glory it is to be inspired and be above the common and natural ways of Knowledge so flatters many Men's Laziness, Ignorance, and Vanity, that when once they are got into this way of immediate Revelation; of Illumination without search; and of certainty without Proof, and without Examination, 'tis a hard matter to get them out of it. (4.19.8)

What is interesting about these sections where Locke characterizes and criticizes enthusiasm in religion is his analysis of the marks and criteria to which these people appeal. Light is said to infuse their understandings, a light that is compared to bright sunshine: it is its own evidence, the truth shows itself (§8). These people "feel the Hand of GOD moving them within". This light from heaven, Locke writes sarcastically, "is strong, clear, and pure, carries its own Demonstration with it, and we may as rationally take a Glow-worme to assist us to discover the Sun, as tc examine the celestial Ray by our dim Candle, Reason" (*ibid.*). What all such talk amounts to is, Locke assures us, that they are sure because they are sure. Take away the metaphors of seeing light and feeling the hand of God, and that is all their claims amount to (§9). To talk of the light of *reason* was apparently acceptable to Locke, but to claim a light from God which bypassed reason (reason being for Locke natural revelation) was suspect. He does not quarrel with the claim that some truths are self-evident. He builds his own theory of knowledge on that notion. What he rejects is using the notion of self-evidence for identifying a truth as a revelation from God (§10). The "Knowledge of any Proposition coming into my Mind, I know not how, is not a Perception that it is from GOD. Much less is a strong Perswasion, that it is true, a Perception that it is from GOD, or so much as true" (*ibid.*). What the enthusiast must "see" is that "it is GOD that reveals" the proposition to him. The criterion question is: "How do I know that GOD is the Revealer of this to me" (*ibid.*). The enthusiast fails to answer this question.

Locke rings the changes on this point in several sections in that chapter of the *Essay* (§10–13). Does he provide an answer to the criterion question? He insists repeatedly that "*Reason* must be our last Judge and Guide in every Thing." (§14). He explains that he does not mean that we should test a proposition said to be revealed by God by seeing if we can discover it to be true by our natural reason. We do not confirm it to be a revelation by confirming its truth. Nevertheless, reason must be consulted in order to determine that some proposition is revealed. Sadly, we are not told how reason does the consulting, or what it looks for, or how it decides. Just when he seems poised to give an answer, he slips in a reference to the Scriptures: if any proposition thought to be revealed conforms to the principles of reason *or* to the "Word of God", we can judge it to be revealed. About the word of God, he says simply, that it is "attested Revelation" (§15). That the phrase "word of God" is meant in this context to be a reference to the Scriptures is clear from two other similar passages which talk of reason and the Scriptures. Just as Locke shied away from producing the demonstrative morality (a morality supposedly derived from reason) and replaced it with instructions to search the Bible for moral truths, so with the criterion for revealed truths he ends by referring to *two* marks or rules by which we can judge that some truths are revealed truths: the rule of reason with its "principles" (which he does not specify) and the rule of the word of God, the Scriptures. What warrants something being a message from heaven is either "the written Word of GOD without us, or that Standard of Reason which is common to us with all Men" (§16).

Could Locke have thought that in describing the Scriptures as being *without* us, they were like the outward and external signs given by God to the men of the Bible as attestations of his revelation? He cites again in section 15 Moses and the burning bush and the rod that turned into a serpent. He says about these prophets of old that they did not conclude to a miracle from some inward feeling or seeing, but had "outward Signs". *These* outward signs functioned in immediate or original revelation. If the Scriptures are taken by Locke as fulfilling the role of an outward sign, of a mark of revelation, they can only function as such in traditional, non-immediate, revelation. It is difficult to determine what it is about the Bible that makes it a sign of being the word of God, since the word, in the sense of the message, cannot in this case be separated from the word, in the sense of the book as an outward sign that the message is from God. What distinguishes the Bible as an historical document from other historical documents is that it was, according to the tradition, in part at least divinely inspired and reports the actions (including the miracles) and sayings of the son of God. The only evidence to support the claim of divine inspiration would seem to be the claims made by some of the writers in that book. Some such as those in the New Testament claim to be reporting first-hand, eye-witnessed events around Jesus, including his signs as being the Son of God. But it would be difficult to believe that Locke means to take their claims as being the outward signs *for us* that God has revealed truths to those men.

No matter how we turn Locke's analysis of the problem of the criterion for revelation (for traditional, not original, revelation). we must finally conclude that he simply accepted the Bible, certainly its New Testament reports of Jesus's life and actions, as true reports of original revelation. Locke's reason, by principles and criteria not specified, convinced him that he should assent to the New Testament story as true revelation. The rationality of Locke's minimalist religion lies in his interpretations of that story, in his textual exegesis of Scriptures, not in any application of his own demands for criteria and signs of revelation extraneous to the truths revealed.

NOTES

1 In *Works* (1823) edn), vol. VI, p. 4. The preface was added by the translator, William Popple.
2 See Phillip Abrams' edition of this (and of a second) early tract, *Two Tracts on Government* (1967), p. 125.
3 For a succinct definition of "magistrate", see Locke's definition in *Two Tracts*: "*By magistrate I understand the supreme legislative power of any society not considering the form of government or number of persons wherein it is placed*" (p. 125). A fuller characterization is given in the second of these tracts, p. 212.
4 In *A Vindication of the Reasonableness of Christianity*, Locke says that atheism is "a crime, which, for its madness as well as guilt, ought to shut a man out of all sober and civil society" (*Works*, 1823 edn, vol. VII, p. 161).
5 *Reasonableness, ibid.*, p. 5.
6 These essays have been edited by W. von Leyden, *Essays on the Law of Nature* (1954). For the reference here, see Lecture IV, pp. 151–5.
7 In *Works* (1823 edn) vol. IX, p. 256. This work was not published in Locke's lifetime. It first appeared in *Posthumous Works* (1706).
8 Biblical commentary and exegesis occupy large portions of *Two Tracts, Two Treatises, Reasonableness, Letter*, and of course the *Paraphrases*.

5

The Metaphysics of Locke's Thought

To my knowledge, no one commented upon Locke's evasiveness over the criterion for revelation. There were, however, challenges to his minimalist Christianity. It must have been the combination of reduction in the doctrines necessary to be believed and some of the newer aspects of his general account of knowledge and reality which gave rise to the strong attack by Edward Stillingfleet, Bishop of Worcester.[1] The play of old orthodoxy against modern views is fascinating to watch in the extended debate between Locke and Stillingfleet. It pits the careful, crafty philosopher against a bishop who was sure of the interpretation of the Bible, a bishop not used to reading the Scriptures in the precise, unprejudiced manner of a man outside the systems of theology. At the time of this debate, Locke had not published his hermeneutical essay on how to read an ancient text, but he had obviously been following the rules and methods he later formulated in that essay whenever he worked over the Bible.[2] Midway through his final reply to Stillingfleet, Locke paused to school the Bishop on how to read the Scriptures.

First, I endeavour to understand the words and phrases of the language I read it in, *i.e.* to form ideas they stand for. If your lordship means any thing else by forming ideas first, I confess I understand it not. And if there be any word or expression, which in that author, or in that place of that author, seems to have a peculiar meaning, i.e. to stand for an idea, which is different from that, which the common use of that language has made it a sign of, that idea also I endeavour to form in my mind, by comparing this author with himself, and observing the design of his discourse, so that, as far as I can, by a sincere endeavour, I may have the same

ideas in every place when I read the words, which the author had
when he writ them. (pp. 341–2)[3]

Very often, too, Locke had to remind the Bishop that what he
and the Church said was in the Bible was not in fact to be found
there: it was interpretation, usually interpretation coloured by
theological bias. Locke's intimate acquaintance with and his
detailed understanding of the Bible is once again on view in his
replies to Stillingfleet.

METAPHYSICS AND THEOLOGY

In his *A Discourse in Vindication of the Doctrine of the Trinity*
(1696), Stillingfleet had charged the *Essay* with containing
doctrines which were antithetical to Christianity, a Christianity as
interpreted by the Church. Locke remarked in his *Second Reply*
that "I read the revelation of the holy Scriptures with a full
assurance that all it delivers is true" (p. 341). He had stated this
claim at the very end of his first response, *A Letter to the Right
Reverend Edward, Lord Bishop of Worcester* (1697):

> The holy scriptures is to me, and always will be, the constant guide
> of my assent; and I shall always hearken to it, as containing
> infallible truth, relating to things of the highest concernment. And
> I wish I could say, there were no mysteries in it: I acknowledge
> there are to me, and I fear always will be. But where I want the
> evidence of things, there yet is ground enough for me to believe,
> because God has said it: and I shall presently condemn and quit
> any opinion of mine, as soon as I am shown that it is contrary to
> any revelation in the holy scripture. But I must confess to your
> lordship, that I do not perceive any such contrariety in any thing in
> my Essay of Human Understanding. (p. 96)

The conflict between Locke and Stillingfleet is a conflict between
the religion of the Scriptures and the religion of the Church or
theologians. Stillingfleet had cited what he took to be definitions
of knowledge in the *Essay* which he felt placed too heavy a
burden on reason and certainty. As we have seen, Locke drew
careful boundaries between belief and knowledge. He did not
answer his own question about the criterion for some assertions

being the revealed word of God but, as he remarked to Stillingfleet in his *Reply* (the second book in this exchange by Locke, not to be confused with his *Second Reply*), "Faith stands by itself, and upon grounds of its own; nor can be removed from them, and placed on those of knowledge" (p. 146). The Bishop claimed he was *certain* of the truths revealed by God, but Locke points out that, unless he confused certainty with the conviction of belief, any belief brought to certainty would cease to be belief (p. 147). The Bible, Locke observes, "speaks of the assurance of faith, but nowhere, that I can remember, of the certainty of faith" (p. 275). The everyday expression, 'I am certain of what I believe', is often linked in the next breath with the claim, 'I know it to be true', but "nobody from thence concludes that believing is knowing" (p. 281).

The disagreements with Stillingfleet were only in part over variant readings of the Scriptures; they were also, on Stillingfleet's part, over Locke's failure to say categorically which doctrines he took to be revealed and which he accordingly accepted. Locke's policy throughout this debate was to cling firmly to what the Scriptures said, not to accept what the Church said they said or implied. There were three doctrines which Stillingfleet defended and tried, unavailingly, to get Locke to admit to: resurrection of the same body, the Trinity, and the immateriality of the soul. The concept of person is at the root of all three, at least as Stillingfleet read Locke.

Nature and Person

Stillingfleet had insisted in his *Discourse* that talking intelligently about the Trinity requires clear and distinct ideas of such terms as 'nature', 'person', 'identity', 'distinction'. He read Locke as saying that these ideas do not come via sensation or reflection, having in mind mainly Locke's remarks about our not knowing the real essence (i.e. the nature) of substances. In his *Letter to the Bishop*, Locke insisted that the phrase 'the nature of man' designates a "collection of several ideas, combined into one complex, abstract idea, which when they are found united in any individual existing, though joined in that existence with other ideas, that individual or particular being is truly said to have the nature of a man" (p. 74). Avoiding the technical sense of 'person' which he had given that term in his *Essay*, Locke gives a common-sense account in his *Letter to the Bishop*. The word 'person' in itself (like all words) has no meaning until we, the users of the word, give it one.

> But as soon as the common use of any language has appropriated it to any idea, then that is the true Idea of a person, and so of nature: but because the propriety of language, *i.e.* the precise idea that every word stands for, is not always exactly known, but is often disputed, there is no other way for him that uses a word that is in dispute, but to define what he signifies by it. (pp. 92–3)

The rejection of any fixed, natural signification to the words in our language is even more forceful in his *Reply*: 'nature' and 'person' get their meaning from "the arbitrary imposition of men" (p. 154). Having made this point about convention in the meaning of our words, Locke might be expected to explain his special sense of 'person', for Stillingfleet stayed with the traditional "individual intelligent substance" definition whereby Peter, James and John were said to share a common nature. Locke does reveal something of his own view about the world when he remarks that "For to speak truly and precisely of this matter, as in reality it is, there is no such thing as one and the same common nature in several individuals; for all that in truth is in them is particular, and can be nothing but particular" (p. 175). He had insisted in his *Essay* that all that exists is particular, there are no *general* natures, general classes, save the genera and classes we form by reference to collections of ideas or qualities.

Stillingfleet seemed to think that because Locke said the word 'person' stood for a complex and abstract *idea*, Locke was saying that there are no persons in the world. The point of Locke's talk of ideas here is simply that it is man who gives meaning to sounds, who turns sounds and shapes into words, but those ideas may also designate particulars in the world which agree with the characteristics identified by the idea. The example he gives in his *Second Reply* is: "he that writes this paper is a person to him, *i.e.* may be denominated a person by him to whose abstract idea of person he bears a conformity" (p. 336). The stress upon the naming and classifying function of man did not, of course, give licence for a frivolous and erratic use of words: "before common use had appropriated that name to that complex idea which they now

signify by the sound person", men could have used what sound
they pleased, but in a country "where those words are already in
common use", the user of the language is obligated to follow the
standard usage (p. 337).

The Trinity

It was the misconstrued reduction of persons to abstract ideas
which, in part, led Stillingfleet to charge Locke's account with
being inadequate to, if not incompatible with, the doctrine of the
Trinity. Stillingfleet's account invoked the concept of substance,
which plays no role in Locke's technical analysis of the person as
a responsible agent of actions. Locke does not in his replies to
Stillingfleet explain the difference between that agent notion of a
person and Stillingfleet's substance view, but Locke does suggest
that the Trinitarian notion of three persons in one substance is
not explicated by the appeal to substance: "where there are three
persons, there must be three distinct, complete, intelligent
substances; and so there cannot be three pesons in the same
individual essence" (p. 338). Locke might have argued that *his*
notion of a person could do more justice to the concept of the
Trinity, for if a person is a function of actions, responsibility, and
consciousness, would that not make it easy to think of the three
persons of the Trinity as three distinct but related persons
through the different areas of activity and responsibility each
covered?[4] Locke was not, however, interested in applying his
concept of a person to this theological doctrine. He wrote his
Essay, he tells Stillingfleet, "without any thought of the controversy between the Trinitarians and Unitarians" (*Letter to the
Bishop*, p. 68). Stillingfleet brought Locke into this dispute
because John Toland, in *Christianity Not Mysterious* (1696),
borrowed doctrines and terminology from Locke's *Essay*. Stillingfleet wanted Locke to tell him whether he believed in the
Trinity or not. Locke refused to give the Bishop any satisfaction,
one way or other: the Trinity was simply beside the point of the
Essay. Whether it was a doctrine Locke accepted (it certainly was
not a necessary doctrine for being a Christian for him), we cannot
tell, since Locke never goes through the Bible to indicate where
the revealed truths are, which ones he does accept as revealed.
His tactic with the Bishop is to argue that his various accounts of

knowledge, certainty, ideas, belief, reason, person have no implications for theology, that Stillingfleet (and Toland) frequently misunderstand what he said, and that the theological language and doctrines invoked by Stillingfleet cannot be found in the Bible.

Resurrection of the Dead

Locke does tell Stillingfleet that "The resurrection of the dead I acknowledge to be an article of the Christian Faith" (p. 303). Where he disagrees is with Stillingfleet's claim that that article refers to the resurrection of the *same* body. We saw earlier how Locke defines same matter (as a set of particles) and same living plant or animal (as particles united by a common life). 'Body' in the exchange here is taken as "material body", and hence refers to the material composition. Locke points out that St Paul says, "you, and not your bodies", when discussing the resurrection (p. 304). Even so, Locke remarks that our body changes through time, the body we have in later years is still our body, but not strictly the *same* body as the one we had earlier:

> your lordship will easily see, that the body he had, when an embryo in the womb, when a child playing in coats, when a man marrying a wife, and when bed-rid, dying of a consumption, and at last, which he shall have after his resurrection; are each of them his body, though neither of them be the same body, the one with the other. (p. 308)

The point Locke is making is simply that "whatever matter is vitally united to his soul, is his body, as much as is that which was united to it when he was born, or in any other part of his life" (p. 314). What is important for the resurrection is that the dead shall rise, that the *person* will be judged. The body is incidental to, though necessary in this life for, the person.

Stillingfleet was not the only one who attacked Locke on this issue. There were many writers who firmly believed that the dead shall rise with the very same bodies they had at death. These writers were not able to separate the agent of action from the bodily vehicle of those actions. There were a number of sermons preached on Easter Sundays on the resurrection of the same body, sermons in which Locke was often attacked. He had some defenders, but by and large, the subtle and important distinction between man and person was lost on his readers. The distinction was lost because of its novelty, but also because of other related doctrines in Locke's *Essay*.

SECULAR METAPHYSICS: TRADITION MODIFIED

In a popular debate at the time between the ancients and moderns – who had contributed most to learning and wisdom? – Locke was clearly on the side of the moderns. He was himself a modern in his language (to which he contributed new words) and in his refusal to follow traditional modes of thought, standard metaphysical categories. Not only did theological doctrines get ignored or received scant attention even when he was writing about religion; in his 'modern' *Essay*, a number of traditional concepts were downgraded, because he showed either that they were speculative concepts without any evidence to support them, or he argued that they were not needed for some of the theological doctrines he did accept. It was this latter feature of the *Essay* which sparked an extensive controversy in the years immediatly following its publication and well into the eighteenth century.

Matter and Thought

Locke accepted the doctrine of the resurrection of the dead and hence of immortality, but he did not believe immortality depended upon the immateriality of the soul. It is doubtful that Locke gave much credence at all to the concept of the soul, although he never rejected it outright. Nor did he ever deny that older notion of immaterial substance. He made the point that the person, the responsible moral agent, was the important item both in this world and in the next. Whether person goes with a soul or substance was of little importance, both because we can have no knowledge of soul or substance and because neither plays any role in action. Hence, the question of whether the soul is material or immaterial was also not very important for Locke. He did profess a conviction that God is immaterial, he mentions other immaterial spirits (e.g. angels), and he does say he believes men also belong on the side of immateriality.

Nevertheless, he made two conceptual points that aroused the orthodox, Stillingfleet among them. The first of these is that, for all we can discover, God could have given to suitably organized and complex matter the property of thought. Since such a linking of thought to matter would seem to eliminate an immaterial soul-substance, Locke remarked that the immortality of persons need not be endangered. If God wants to resurrect us, he will do so, whether we are material or immaterial subtances. Whether Locke was foolhardy, courageous, or just coolly rational in this suggestion about God being able to make thought a property of matter, he incurred the enmity of a wide variety of people. To make matters worse, materialism was seen as a near-present danger: Hobbes and Spinoza had been branded with that label; there were lesser figures who also flirted in that direction. Ralph Cudworth (the father of Locke's friend Damaris Masham) had in 1678 published a large volume, *The True Intellectual System of the Universe*, detailing the various forms of materialism among the ancients, intending this inventory and analysis as a warning for the moderns not to be tempted.

Some of Locke's readers (e.g. Thomas Long[5]) saw his call for wide toleration as a cover for Jesuitical infiltration; others saw his stress on rationality in religion as another move in the direction of the newer forms of religion which the more tradition-bound believers viewed as irreligion; his remark about immateriality not being necessary for immortality and his suggestion of thought being compatible with a certain kind of matter (e.g. the brain) simply reinforced the fears of many of his contemporaries that the doctrines of this man were a full-scale attack on – certainly a threat to – established beliefs. The incipient materialism some saw in these suggestions about thought and matter challenged even more fundamental beliefs about the nature of the world and God's role in creation: Locke was considered as changing, if not eliminating, the very concept of substance.

In responding to Stillingfleet's alarm over the *Essay* suggestion of God adding thought to matter, Locke clarified for the Bishop that he was not suggesting that thought is a *natural* property of matter, a 'natural' property being one which expresses the nature of a substance, even an essential property (p. 468). Locke accepted the standard corpuscular definition of matter, as extended, solid, inert, passive corpuscles. But the question is: is God's power limited to adding only natural properties to matter? In creating extended, solid substance, has God foreclosed changing some of its other properties, or even adding new ones?

> The idea of matter is an extended solid substance; wherever there is such a substance, there is matter, and the essence of matter, whatever other qualities, not contained in that essence, it shall please God to superadd to it. For example, God creates an extended solid substance, without the superadding any thing else to it, and so we may consider it at rest: to some parts of it he superadds motion, but it has still the essence of matter: other parts of it he frames into plants, with all the excellencies of vegetation, life, and beauty, which are to be found in a rose or a peach-tree, &c. above the essence of matter in general, but it is still but matter: to other parts he adds sense and spontaneous motion, and those other properties that are to be found in an elephant. (p. 460)

Locke wants to know why this process cannot be taken one step further, where God adds thought to some of this matter. It would still be matter, albeit thinking matter. The idea of matter having the properties of extension *and* thought was incomprehensible to most orthodox thinkers of that time. Not only did it sound to them like materialism, for it seemed to imply only *one* substance (just as Spinoza said) with immaterial substance eliminated; it appeared as well to undermine the very notion of substance.[6]

Substance

It was this latter charge, that he had taken substance out of the world, had eliminated the concept of substance from his account, which was the basic charge levelled by Stillingfleet. The reliance upon the categories of substance, mode and property was shared by most people; it marked the familiar and comfortable conceptual account of the world. The way people thought about ordinary, physical objects, e.g. a horse or a stone, was, in Locke's description of this standard view, as "the Complication, or Collection of several simple *Ideas* of sensible Qualities" which are discovered to go together, and which, "because we cannot conceive, how they should subsist alone, nor one in another, we suppose them existing in, and supported by some common subject" (*Essay*, 2.23.4). We speak of a white horse, of a hard stone, where the quality is taken to belong to something – the horse or the stone. The same conception holds for those properties associated with "the Operations of the Mind", properties such as thinking, reasoning, willing, fearing: these too, we normally believe, cannot "subsist of themselves" but must belong to some object, to a mind, a person, a soul (2.23.5). The subject to which these properties or qualities belong was thought of as a substance. Substances have qualities, some essential, some accidental or contingent. Essential, natural properties define the substance: it is a thinking thing, it is an extended thing. Qualities and properties require a subject, a substance; they cannot exist by themselves. Red requires a thing which is red, thinking requires a thing which thinks.

Talking about qualities and properties is easy enough, they are open to observation and reflection. Part of good science for Locke was refining our observations of objects or events and our reflections on ourselves so that we could be more detailed and more precise about what qualities regularly go together and what relations they have to each other and to other groups of qualities. If we attempt to talk about the *subject* of the observed qualities and properties, e.g. the horse, all we seem able to say is something about the other properties of the horse: his speed, his size, whose horse he is, where he grazes. The same situation applies to more general objects such as gold, silver, or lead (the objects chemists, such as Locke's friend, Robert Boyle, were interested in). The analysis of gold or lead resulted in the discovery of how it behaved in the fire, in certain solutions, in light, etc., the qualities it manifests in those situations: does it melt, dissolve, is it opaque, hard, with a certain heaviness? The 'it' of the analysis seems to escape our observation and experiments.

At first glance, it may seem that we are better off with immaterial substances, the subject of those properties of thinking, knowing, doubting, believing, etc., for we can say it is Jones who thinks, wills, believes, etc. But what is our account of Jones? He is he who thinks, but besides a long, perhaps indefinite, list of other properties, what can we say about Jones? What *is* Jones? The answer comes round again: 'the subject who thinks', or, to use the language of Locke's contemporaries, 'the substratum of the operations of thinking, willing, etc.'. In comparing the ideas we can obtain of the properties and operations of bodies and of persons, Locke pointed out the detail, precision and clarity of our ideas of properties, and the vague, almost empty content of our ideas of substances.

> We have as clear a Notion of the Substance of Spirit [mind or soul], *as we have of Body*; the one being supposed to be (without knowing what it is) the *Substratum* to those simple *Ideas* we have from without; and the other supposed (with a like ignorance of what it is) to be the *Substratum* to those Operations, which we experiment in our selves within. (2.23.5)

The conclusion Locke draws from these remarks about our ideas of substance and qualities is as follows:

> Whatever therefore be the secret and abstract Nature of *Substance* in general, all *the* Ideas *we have of particular distinct sorts of Substances*, are nothing but several Combinations of simple *Ideas*, coexisting in such, though unknown, Cause of their Union, as makes the whole subsist of itself. (2.23.6)

The question was, how seriously did Locke accept both parts of this conclusion, the ideas or qualities and that in which those qualities were said to subsist? Does the use of the word 'suppose' (which occurs frequently in his account), "which he supposes to inhere, with a supposition of such a *Substratum*", indicate more than an uneasiness with the notion of substance? Stillingfleet felt it did. It did not help convince the Bishop of Locke's commitment to substance when he dropped the term out of some of his accounts: "Thus the *Idea* of the *Sun*, What is it, but an aggregate of those several simple *Ideas*, Bright, Hot, Roundish, having a constant regular motion, at a certain distance from us, and, perhaps, some other" (2.23.6). Nor did it satisfy the Bishop to have Locke (in his *Letter to the Bishop*) distinguish between the *being* and the *idea* of substance: "I ground not the being, but the idea of substance, on our accustoming ourselves to suppose some substratum" (p. 18).

As in religious doctrines, so with this metaphysical concept of substance, Stillingfleet wanted Locke to say we are certain of the being of substance. Locke does gradually move closer and closer to saying just that. He speaks the traditional language when he says that the ideas of qualities, action and powers "are perceived by the mind to be by themselves inconsistent with existence" (p. 21). He even says that "the mind perceives their necessary connexion with inherence or being supported". By the time Locke is into his third and final response (*Second Reply*), he even says: "For I held we might be certain of the truth of this proposition, that there was substance in the world" (p. 236). In two other passages, he becomes even more emphatic: "the idea of substance is clear and distinct enough to have its agreement with that of actual existence perceived" (p. 241), and "I am certain, that I have evident knowledge, that the substance of my body and soul exists, though I am as certain that I have but a very obscure and confused idea of any substance at all" (p. 345).

Perhaps Locke was goaded into this admission after these long exchanges, although he does not seem to have been a man easily goaded. Perhaps he really did accept the metaphysics of substance and quality. There may be a parallel between his religion and his metaphysics: just as he may have believed more truths in the Bible than the few necessary for being a Christian, so he may have accepted more metaphysical doctrines and conceptual categories than he thought necessary for science, action and morality. What he finds we can discover about persons and objects, what he thinks we need for morality and science, may be less than what he accepted among the conceptual tools of his predecessors. Despite his claim to Stillingfleet that he does accept the existence of substance, he employs that concept hardly at all in his account of man and person, nor does he use that concept in the traditional way when talking about ordinary objects. He may have been equivocating in his admission to Stillingfleet, for when we examine the *Essay* chapter, "Of our Complex Ideas of Substances" (2.23), as well as "Of the Names of Substances" (3.6), we find a common-sense and a chemical (not a metaphysical) use of the term "substances', which may have been what Locke had in mind in his response to the Bishop.

Essence

In those discussions, the substances cited include man, horse, stone, water, ice, gold, iron, diamond. It is what Locke refers to as the *"Notion of pure Substance in general"* (2.23.2) which is the substratum concept, the idea which is obscure and unclear. The individual substances, the objects of everyday life, are not *substance* in this sense. Part of the traditional idea of substance contained the notion of support, of underlying the qualities, that which is over and above the qualities. The other part of that traditional idea relates to talk of essence. 'Essence' *is* a traditional term Locke employs extensively, but he adapts it to his own purposes, one component of it filling a role in his account of classification and another applying it to the current scientific hypothesis of corpuscular matter.

In adapting the term 'essence' to his purposes, Locke gives an inventory of that term's use in instruction in the Schools, a use transmitted by the standard logic manuals. The first meaning is "for the very being of any thing, whereby it is, what it is"(*Essay*, 3.3.15). Translated into the terminology used by Locke, this sense of 'essence' is "the real internal, but generally in Substance, unknown Constitution of Things, whereon their discoverable Qualities depend". The second meaning of the term is its application to the "artificial Constitution of *Genus* and *Species*", in contrast to the real, natural internal constitution. Locke's view of classification, a view shared by some other writers, is that "Things are ranked under Names into sorts or *Species*, only as they agree to certain abstract *Ideas*", and thus essence is just the abstract idea "which the General, or *Sortal* . . . Name stands for". This second sense of 'essence' can accordingly be called the 'nominal essence', in contrast with the first sense, the 'real essence'.

There were two interpretations of the real essence. One says there are only "a certain number of those Essences, according to which, all natural things are made, and wherein they do exactly every one of them partake", a limited number of fixed, natural species (3.3.17). The other interpretation (the more rational one, Locke says) takes the real essence to be the internal constitution of the insensible parts (the corpuscles) of the object, "from which flow those sensible Qualities, which serve us to distinguish them one from another, according as we have Occasion to rank them into sorts, under common Denominations" (under the nominal essence). The first interpretation of 'real essence', in terms of fixed species, "Forms or Molds, wherein all natural Things, that exist, are cast", has been detrimental to the advancement of science. There are as well phenomena which show this interpretation to be false (e.g. the production of monsters, "Changelings, and other strange Issues of humane Birth"), but his main objection is that it makes an unknown essence the means for distinguishing "the Species of Things". The only useful basis for classification is one designed to fit our purposes, based upon what we discover about properties and the behaviour of things.

Particulars

The 'things' that make up Locke's world are particulars. It is to his concept of *particular things* that we must look in order to understand this aspect of the metaphysics of Locke's thought. It is in the account of particulars that he breaks most markedly with tradition. Particulars, what he sometimes calls 'particular beings', when "considered barely in themselves" apart from the uses we put them to and the classifications we use, will be found to have all their "Qualities equally *essential*; and every thing, in each individual, will be *essential* to it, or, which is more true, nothing at all" (3.6.5). When not being considered by us as a kind of thing, gold, or that "individual parcel of Matter" which we call 'gold', has none of its qualities essential and inseparable from it (3.6.6). A more striking example to illustrate this point is a particular man.

> 'Tis necessary for me to be as I am; GOD and Nature has made me so: But there is nothing I have, is essential to me. An Accident, or Disease, may very much alter my Colour, or Shape; a Fever, or Fall, may take away my Reason, or Memory, or both; and an Apoplexy leave neither Sense, nor Understanding, no nor Life. (3.6.4)

The term 'essence' relates to sorts, there are no sorts in nature (only particulars), thus, 'essence' is a term of art devised by man to enable us to refer to and identify similar groups of properties. Thus, to take the example of man again,

> For to talk of a *Man*, and to lay by, at the same time, the ordinary signification of the Name Man, which is our complex *Idea*, usually annexed to it; and bid the Reader consider *Man*, as he is in

himself, and as he is really distinguished from others, in his internal Constitution, or real Essence, that is, by something, he knows not what, looks like trifling: and yet thus one must do, who would speak of the supposed real Essences and *Species* of Things, as thought to be made by Nature. (3.6.43)

This last quotation reminds us that Locke does have a concept of real essence, that is, of the internal constitution of every particular. A knowledge of the internal constitution of man (presumably, of the biological and corpuscular – genetic, today – constitution), the constitution from which "his Faculties of Moving, Sensation, and Reasoning, and other Powers flow; and on which his so regular shape depends, as 'tis possible Angels have, and 'tis certain his Maker has", gives us "a quite other *Idea* of his *Essence*, than what now is contained in our Definition of that *Species*" (3.6.3). We shall discover later that the idea of man's essence which God and angels have differs in being non-observational, derived immediately from the knowledge they have of the internal constitution, and hence being complete rather than, as ours is, selective and partial. The partial and incomplete nature of our knowledge of particulars is illustrated by the discovery chemists frequently make of unexpected qualities in substances they classify as of the same sort, e.g. when they seek in vain "for the same Qualities in one parcel of Sulphur, Antimony, or Vitriol, which they have found in others" (3.6.8). A substance which chemists classify under the same name is often found to have qualities "as far different one from another, as from others, from which they are accounted to differ *specifically*". Yet, according to Locke's account of particulars, all of the qualities of these substances, both those they share with other substances ranked by us in the same class and those ranked in different classes, depend upon "their real Constitutions".

On Locke's account of particulars, everyone "has its peculiar Constitution, whereon depend those sensible Qualities, and Powers, we observe" in them (3.6.13). He even suggests that that peculiar internal constitution "which every Thing has within it self" is had "without any relation to any thing without it" (3.6.6), a suggestion which may not be entirely consistent with some remarks he makes elsewhere, which we shall consider in a moment. The particularity of objects does not ignore the fact of similarities, similarities in many sensible qualities, but "probably too, in their internal frame and Constitution" (3.6.36). The "agreement and likeness" which 'nature' has given to "many particular Substances" affords a "Foundation of being ranked into sorts" (3.6.30). But our ranking into sorts is limited to *observed* similarities; even though observed qualities are based upon and are a function of the "internal Nature of the Things", our knowledge not extending to the internal nature, our classification will hardly be adequate to the internal nature (3.6.37).

This chapter of the *Essay* is filled with numerous examples of arbitrary classifications fitted to our purposes. There are other examples which show that our classifications are not natural ones, they do not arise from the internal nature of objects, only from their qualities as determined relevant by us. The irrelevance of the internal constitution of particulars to their classification is illustrated by comparison with artificial objects, where the internal structure *is known*.

> There are some *Watches*, that are made with four Wheels, others with five: Is this a specifick difference to the Workman? Some have Strings and Physies [i.e., wheels], and others none; some have the Balance loose, and others regulated by a spiral Spring, and others by Hogs Bristles: Are any, or all of these enough to make a specifick difference to the Workman, that knows each of these, and several other different contrivances, in the internal Constitution of *Watches*? 'Tis certain, each of these hath a real difference from the rest: But whether it be an essential, a specifick difference or no, relates only to the complex *Idea*, to which the name *Watch* is given. (3.6.39)

Similarly,

> No body will doubt, that the Wheels, or Springs (if I may so say) within, are different in a *rational Man*, and a *Changeling*. no more than that there is a difference in the frame between a *Drill* and a *Changeling*. But whether one, or both these differences be essential, or specifical, is only to be known to us, by their agreement, or disagreement with the complex *Idea* that the name *Man* stands for. (*ibid.*)

There is no indication of what the "Wheels, or Springs" of man and animals might be. Presumably Locke did not mean this to relate to his suggestion about thought being made a property of matter; only that the physiology of nerves and brain, cited often by him, was either different or functioned differently in man and changelings. What is important is his frequent remark that we do not have access to the internal mechanism of the 'machine of the body', just as our access to inorganic matter is restricted to observed qualities from which we form the nominal essence of a class into which we place individuals.

There was for Locke a close similarity between the conventional aspect of our generic or class names and the conventional nature of language generally. As well, those mixed modes which were archetypes for actions carry this same non-natural conventionality. Man is very active in defining and characterizing his world, both the social and the physical, largely because certain aspects of the world are inaccessible to him. Just as the presence of innate truths in our minds would result in universal recognition of the same truths, so were our class terms the result of "Nature's Workmanship, they could not be so various and different in several Men, as experience tells us they are" (3.6.26).

Nominal essences, the collections of qualities shared by several particulars, enable us to sort the particulars composing Locke's world into categories and classes suitable to our needs. These particulars have an internal, hidden structure which accounts for and causes the observable qualities of each particular. In saying in one passage that each particular has an internal structure "without any relation to any thing without it" (3.6.6), Locke appears to contradict a later claim in Book Four, that "however absolute and entire" things "seem in themselves", they are "but Retainers to other parts of Nature" (4.6.11). He even goes on to say that the "observable Qualities, Actions, and Powers" of objects "are owing to something without them", when so many passages in Book Three, Chapter Six claimed that the observable qualities flow from the internal structure of each particular. This section goes to extended lengths to suggest ways in which both organic and inorganic objects are dependent upon their environment and other objects, both near and distant. Some parts of this fascinating passage are conjecture, other parts simply call attention to the dependence of plants and animals on the "extrinsical Causes and Qualities of other Bodies" for their life and motion. But the picture of the world suggested in this 4.6 section is one of tight and pervasive interconnection of parts and whole, and of parts to each other.

While the picture is not quite the same as that found in a 3.6 passage, the similarities are important for reaching an understanding of the metaphysics of Locke's thought. I refer to 3.6.12, where he details what was commonly accepted as the scale or chain of being. The passage starts off by reminding us of the limitations of our knowledge: "It is not impossible to conceive, nor repugnant to reason, that there may be many *Species of Spirits*, as much separated and diversified one from another by distinct Properties, whereof we have no *Ideas*." He offers as a probable opinion that there are "more Species of intelligent Creatures above us, than there are of sensible and material below us". The probability of this opinion is supported by what Locke offers as a fact: "That in all the visible corporeal World, we see no Chasms, or Gaps". In some writers, the scale of being is taken as a scale of kinds, where the difference between species is gradual, with overlapping characteristics. As Locke says: "All quite down from us, the descent is by easy steps, and a continued series of Things, that in each remove, differ very little one from the other". In Locke's world, where all that exists is particular, and where there are no natural kinds, the account should only be in terms of overlapping properties, but he does sometimes write as if he is talking of real species; the "several Species are linked together, and differ but in almost insensible degrees." The particulars do form a descending and an ascending scale from and towards perfection, God being the highest point on the scale.

His examples of shared species or shared properties in this passage are interesting:

1 "Fishes that have Wings, and are not Strangers to the Airy Region."
2 "Birds, that are Inhabitants of the Water; whose Blood is cold as Fishes, and their Flesh so like in taste, that the scrupulous are allow'd them on Fish-days."
3 "Amphibious Animals link the Terrestrial and Aquatique together; Seals live at Land and at Sea, and Porpoises have the warm Blood and Entrails of a Hog, not to mention what is confidently reported of Mermaids, or Sea-Men."
4 "Brutes that seem to have as much Knowledge and Reason, as some that are called Men."

There are other examples of cross-species (or mixed class properties) cited by Locke when he is calling into question the reality of natural classes. These examples also seem to fill out his notion of the chain of being, at least in showing the filling-in of gaps.

5 "Creatures in the World, that have shapes like ours, but are hairy, and want Language, and Reason" (3.6.22).
6 "Naturals amongst us, that have perfectly our shape, but want Reason, and some of them Language too" (*ibid.*).
7 Creatures "that with Language, and Reason, and a shape in other Things agreeing with ours, have hairy Tails" (*ibid.*).
8 Other creatures "where the Males have no Beards, and others where the Females have" (*ibid.*).
9 He also tells of reports of women conceiving by Drills (3.6.23).
10 In citing the examples of mules (the issue of an Ass and a Mare) and Gimars (the mixture of a Bull and a Mare), he says: "I once saw a Creature, that was the Issue of a Cat and a Rat, and had the plain Marks of both about it." (*ibid.*).
11 He says that "it has been more than once debated, whether several humane *Foetus* should be preserved, or received to Baptism, or no, only because of the difference of their outward Configuration, from the ordinary Make of Children" (3.6.26). The Abbot of St Martin is cited, who had "so little of the Figure of a Man" when he was born that people took him to be a monster and debated for a while whether to baptize him.

Locke's citation of these various mixings of species can be confusing if we take him to be saying that there are no regularities in nature, that anything may issue from any biological coupling. The examples he gives (and apparently believes) are unusual, exceptions to what normally happens. Locke is reluctant to accept the notion that there is a human nature which we all share or exemplify, because this seemed to him to lead to a metaphysical notion he did reject: that there are fixed forms or moulds (ontological classes) which determine what exists, at least in the biological world. He viewed this metaphysical notion as similar to the notion of substance: neither is explanatory and neither gives us any clear idea of what is being invoked. For physical matter and material objects, it was the corpuscular hypothesis which offered the best explanation of the bodies we know through experience. The corpuscular hypothesis, as formulated by

Locke's friend Robert Boyle, explained the qualities of objects, and their behaviour, by reference to the motion and structure of insensible corpuscles. Corpuscularity presumably also applies to living bodies (plants and animals), but it will not account for or explain all or even the most important aspects of such bodies. Locke's metaphor referring to the "wheels or springs" of man and animals indicates his recognition that more than insensible corpuscles are involved. Other passages refer to and use the physiology of his contemporaries, a physiology of nerves as tubes with fluids, of muscles made to expand and contract by the flow of that nervous fluid (i.e. what was called 'animal spirits'). The 'life' of biological organisms was in part a result of these ingredients in the machine of the body. Since Locke's references to wheels or springs in that 3.6.39 passage was to *rational* man, that metaphor very likely also included *mental* causes as well. Volition is a mover of men; animal spirits, nerves and muscles move bodies.

In rejecting natural classes and insisting that all that exists is particular, Locke was trying to direct attention upon the internal mechanism of bodies, to corpuscles for inanimate bodies, to neurophysiology for living bodies. Most of his attention is given to the former and to the corpuscular theory, but we should not ignore the several passages where the physiology of our bodies is used (e.g. 2.1.15; 2.8.4,12,21; 2.10.5,9; 2.27.13,27; 2.33.6; 4.10.9).

CAUSES AS POWERS

In both animate and inanimate bodies, the relation between the internal mechanism and outward appearances or behaviour is causal. The most general definition of 'cause' for Locke is "that which makes any other thing, either simple *Idea*, Substance, or Mode, begin to be" (*Essay*, 2.26.2). Different types of causal action are identified. "When the thing is wholly made new, so that no part thereof did ever exist before; or when a new Particle of Matter doth begin to exist, *in rerum natura*, which had before no Being, and this we call *Creation*." When separate particles are united in new ways, thereby resulting in something which had not existed before (e.g. this man, this egg, this rose), we call that 'generation'. Locke's quick account of the process of generation refers to "an internal Principle": when a man, an egg, a rose is "produced in the ordinary course of Nature, by an internal Principle, but set on work by, and received from some external Agent, or Cause, and working by insensible ways, which we perceive not". Other types of causation are designated 'making' and 'alteration': "Thus a Man is generated, a Picture made, and either of them altered, when any new sensible Quality, or simple *Idea*, is produced in either of them, which was not there before". To acquire the idea of cause we do not need to know "the manner of that operation" which creates, generates, or alters. Too much effort spent in trying to "penetrate into the Causes of Things", can lead us to accept hypotheses too hastily without solid foundation (4.12.13). We see all sorts of changes and productions: "Animals are generated, nourished, and [we see them] move"; we see "the parts of a Candle successively melting"; and we witness the loadstone attracting iron (4.16.12). But "the causes that operate, and the manner they are produced in, we can only guess, and probably conjecture." That there are "regular proceedings of Causes and Effects in the ordinary course of Nature", he firmly accepts (4.16.6).

Cause is closely linked with power. It is by observing change and alteration, coming into existence and ceasing to exist, as well as our reflection on the change and flow of ideas and thoughts in our mind, that we come to the dual notion of the possibility of being changed and of making change. This dual idea is the idea of power (2.21.1). *Active* and *passive* powers are involved in all the types of cause. There is some mild hesitation on Locke's part to credit active powers to matter, since this would have been a radical claim at that time. Newton had, in his 1687 *Principia Mathematica*, fought shy of the same claim, insisting that the *forces* of attraction and repulsion (gravity) were not *natural* powers of matter, but only powers added by God. Newton, and most of his and Locke's contemporaries, preferred to limit active power to God, and perhaps to other spirits such as man. While Locke does believe we can acquire a clear and distinct idea of active power from "reflection on the Operations of our Minds", and while he says that body does not furnish us with any idea of "the beginning of Motion" (2.21.4), he does claim that "*active Powers* make so great a part of our complex *Ideas* of natural

Substances" (2.21.2). The passage where he entertains the possibility that God might, besides motion, also add thought to matter, speaks of the "natural Powers of Matter", although he insists that thought is not one of those (4.3.6). Passive powers can also be natural, so we should not too quickly see this reference as one to natural active powers.

That the concept of power is an important one for Locke's account of objects (i.e. substances), is evident whenever he discusses their qualities. Frequently, he speaks of "the Qualities, and Powers of Substances", or he will say that "The simple *Ideas* whereof we make our complex ones of Substances, are all of them (bating only the Figure and Bulk of some sorts) Powers" (2.31.8). This last remark goes on to explain that those powers are "Relations to other Substances", reminding us of that passage about the interconnection of all things. Listed among the powers of gold are colour and weight, the first being a power to affect our eyes, the other the power "to force upwards any other Body of equal bulk" (2.31.9). That these are only *passive* powers is suggested by his going on to cite 'fusibility' and 'fixedness' as "two other passive powers, in relation to the operation of fire". 'Ductility' and 'solubility' are also cited as powers. The chapter *"Of Our Ideas of Substances"* says unequivocally that our ideas of substances contain both "active Powers, and passive Capacities", the "power of drawing Iron" being an active power correlated with the passive power of "being so drawn" (2.23.7). A later remark speaks of "the Active and Passive Powers of Bodies", tracing them both to the "Texture and Motion of Parts" (4.3.16). Heat and colour of fire is said to be "nothing but Powers in it, to produce those *Ideas* in us" (2.23.7). Another active power of fire is the ability to change wood into charcoal, i.e. "to change the colour and consistency of Wood". The power of gold to be melted is a passive power, as is its power of "being dissolved in *Aqua Regia*" (2.23.10). The heat we feel from the sun, and the white colour which the sun produces in wax, are both powers in the sun "operating, by the Motion and Figure of its insensible Parts, so on a Man, as to make him have the *Idea* of Heat; and so on Wax, as to make it capable to produce in a Man the *Idea* of White".

The chapter which details an account of the qualities of bodies (2.8) draws a distinction between two main types: primary qualities, such as the bulk, number, figure and motion of the particles, and another sort which are only powers, the power to produce ideas in perceivers, and the power to change the qualities of other objects. The first sort of powers (what he calls 'secondary qualities') is a function of the primary qualities of its insensible particles operating "after a peculiar manner on any of our Senses" (2.8.23). The second sort of powers (what he sometimes calls "*Secondary Qualities, mediately perceivable*": 2.8.26) are a function of the particular constitution of a body's primary qualities. The active powers are, then, a function of the insensible corpuscles: Locke describes these as "the active parts of Matter, and the great Instruments of Nature" (4.3.25).

The theme that the internal mechanism, the wheels and springs, of physical objects is causally responsible for the sensible ideas we have of them is a recurring one throughout the *Essay*. Whether we can say that the active powers which he seems to ascribe to matter and to bodies were active in the full sense is a bit difficult to say. There are strong remarks which seem to support such a conclusion, but there are also passages, important ones, where he issues warnings. At the end of the chapter on power (2.21), he warns us not to be misled by the grammar of active verbs: not every such verb really designates a genuine action (2.21.72). There are instances of thinking and motion (the two concepts of action) which are not actions proper, only passions, the receiving of some action from something external. Genuine action is self-generated, self-initiated motion. It is only when some substance or agent "puts it self into *Action* by its own Power" that we have real active power at work. Hence the importance for Locke of the agency of the person.

Locke did not profess to understand the causation of bodies or of persons, but he did insist that for bodies, "we cannot conceive any thing else, to be in any sensible Object, whereby it produces different *Ideas* in us, but the different Bulk, Figure, Number, Texture, and Motion of its insensible Parts" (2.21.73). When it comes to a consideration of the active powers of men as agents of action, that power is not, or is not entirely, a function of corpuscles or of physiology. In the chapter on power, a chapter which received numerous revisions and additions over several editions, he speaks of a power we find in ourselves "to begin or forbear, continue or end several actions of our mind, and motions of our Bodies" (2.21.5). The power is traced to thought and volition, the mind is spoken of as being able to 'command' "the doing or not doing such or such a particular action". Freedom is characterized in those terms:

> All the Actions, that we have any *Idea* of, reducing themselves, as has been said, to these two, *viz*. Thinking and Motion, so far as a Man has a power to think, or not to think; to move, or not to move, according to the preference or direction of his own mind, so far is a Man *Free*. Where-ever any performance or forbearance are not equally in a Man's power; where-ever doing or not doing, will not equally follow upon the preference of his mind directing it, there he is not *Free*, though perhaps the Action may be voluntary. (2.21.8)

CONCLUSION

Power, whether that of persons to be free agents or the various powers of objects, turns out to be an important ingredient in Locke's account of the world. Power is always the power of some *particular*, a particular object or a particular person. He does not clarify just how he thought his talk of the interconnection of all objects was consistent with his talk of the qualities of objects 'flowing from' the internal corpuscular structure of those objects. One way to make these two strands in his thought consistent is to say that *active* power, self-initiating power, is only found outside the causal network of physical power of objects (what he terms "*Mobility*, or the Power of being moved": 2.21.73), reserving active powers (the power of perception or thinking, 'perceptivity', and the power of moving, 'motivity': 2.21.73) to agents or persons. That we *acquire the ideas* of perceptivity and motivity from reflecting on *ourselves* is a claim Locke does make in several passages. The traditional, orthodox doctrine about matter was that it is passive and inert. That orthodoxy also found the only pure form of active power in God, with some allowance for lesser spirits such as man to be able, as in free action, to initiate new motions, to add (almost as in creation) new ingredients to the world.

Locke was quickly read by his contemporaries and immediate successors as assigning active powers to matter, especially, for those who found materialism in his thought, the active power of perceptivity. With so many traditional fundamental concepts and doctrines challenged by what Locke did say, as well as what, to the consternation of Stillingfleet, he left unsaid, it should be no surprise that he was seen as anticipating the direction in which the Newtonians were going: making matter active. Locke preferred to get along with fewer metaphysical concepts rather than more. Just as he was a minimalist in religion (in the doctrines necessary for being a Christian), so he endorsed a minimalist metaphysics, eliminating as many of the older categories as he could. Most often, his professed reason for elimination was that some term or concept had no basis in our experience, even though, as with 'substance', he recognized the natural tendency we have of referring qualities to some subject. There was also, I think, an aspect of his character which pushed him towards simpler systems of thought.

NOTES

1 See his *A Discourse in Vindication of the Doctrine of the Trinity*, 1696. He published two additional attacks on Locke, in 1697 and 1698, as responses to Locke's various replies.
2 See Locke's 'An Essay for the Understanding of St. Paul's Epistles', the preface to his *A Paraphrase and Notes on the Epistles of St. Paul* (1705–07), reprinted in *Works* (1823 edn), vol. VIII.
3 *Mr. Locke's Reply to the . . . Bishop of Worcester's . . . Second Letter* (1699). Locke's first response to Stillingfleet carried the title *Letter to the Right Reverend Edward, Lord Bishop of Worcester* (1697). The second response was *Mr. Locke's Reply to the . . . Bishop of Worcester* (1697). These are all reprinted in *Works*, (1823 edn) vol. IV, pp. 1–96, 97–189 and 191–498 respectively.
4 William Sherlock, who did try such an explication, got into theological trouble. See his *A Vindication of the Doctrine of the Holy and Ever Blessed Trinity* (1690). Robert South attacked Sherlock in several tracts, *Animadversions upon Dr. Sherlock's Book* (1693), and *Tritheism Charged upon Dr. Sherlock's New Notion of the Trinity* (1695).
5 See Long's *The Letter for Toleration Decipher'd* (1689).
6 I have recently traced the controversy raised by Locke in Britain over his suggestion about God adding thought to matter. See my *Thinking Matter* (1984).

6

The Science of Mind

The concluding section to the long chapter on power in the *Essay* (in its final revision, this chapter ran to 73 sections, by far the longest chapter in that book) draws a distinction between "the Knowledge the mind has of Things, by those *Ideas*, and Appearances, which *God* has fitted it to receive from them", and the "Causes, or manner of Production" of those ideas and appearances. To "enquire philosophically [i.e. scientifically] into the peculiar Constitution of Bodies, and the Configuration of Parts, whereby they have the power to produce in us *Ideas* of their sensible Qualities" would be, he there says, "contrary to the Design of this Essay". Despite the fact that by the time he reaches this chapter in Book 2 he has made frequent references to the physical genesis of ideas and appearances, as well as invoking the concept of natural powers in matter, Locke draws, at the beginning of the *Essay*, a similar distinction between knowledge and causes. He describes the design of the *Essay* in 1.1.2 as: "to enquire into the Original, Certainty, and Extent of humane Knowledge; together with the Grounds and Degrees of Belief, Opinion, and Assent". He says that he will not *at present* "meddle with the Physical Consideration of the Mind". Besides not undertaking a scientific examination of the causes of thought, Locke disavows several speculative questions about the mind:

> wherein its Essence consists, or by what Motions of our Spirits [animal spirits], or Alterations of our Bodies, we come to have any Sensation by our Organs, or any *Ideas* in our Understandings; and whether those *Ideas* do in their Formation, any, or all of them, depend on Matter, or no. These are Speculations, which, however curious and entertaining, I shall decline, as lying out of my Way, in the Design I am now upon.

Both speculative and causal theories, however, continued to intrigue him. That same section 73 offers an outline of a physical explication of our ideas. That explication, were Locke able to make it, would supplement the psychological explication he has given in the early chapters of Book 2. Were he to consider and examine "on what Causes" our ideas depend, and "of what they are made", he would find, he says, eight basic ideas in terms of which all the others could be explicated physically. These eight ideas are listed in three groups. The first group contains extension, solidity and mobility. We are said to receive these three ideas from bodies, by means of our senses. The second group consists of perceptivity and motivity, which are received "from our Minds", i.e. from attending to ourselves when we perceive and move. The third group of basic ideas contains three more: existence, duration and number. These last three are said to belong to the ideas in the other two groups. As a hint of how these eight basic and original ideas could explain other ideas, Locke speculates:

> I imagine, [from these eight] might be explained the nature of Colours, Sounds, Tastes, Smells, and all other *Ideas* we have, if we had but Faculties acute enough to perceive the severally modified Extensions, and Motions, of these minute Bodies, which produce those several Sensations in us. (2.21.73)

This classification of ideas reveals Locke's Cartesian background, for it is, save for a minor change of vocabulary, identical with a classification Descartes gave. In a letter to Princess Elizabeth, dated 21 May 1643, Descartes addressed the question of how we can conceive the soul and body to interact. He says that "there are in us certain primitive notions which are as it were models on which all our other knowledge is patterned".[1] He then groups these primitive notions as those which relate to the body (extension, shape and movement) and those which relate to the soul (thought, or the intellect and the inclinations of the will). The third group are described as general ones, pertaining to both groups: being, number and duration.[2] Descartes used this classification of basic ideas to try to explain how the soul acts on the body and the body acts on the soul. Whether or not he is successful in his explantion, it is instructive to discover that both he and Locke use a similar classification for roughly the same purposes. Locke's explication, however, is mainly physical, in terms of the corpuscular theory of matter. Both writers viewed the classification as one of ideas or appearances, distinguishing them from their causes.

LOCKE'S METHOD: ITS RELATION TO SCIENCE AND LOGIC

It is this distinction between appearances and their physical causes which identifies Locke's main objective in his *Essay*. He was not much concerned, as he said, with the physical origin of these appearances, but he clearly did accept the prevailing account in terms of the corpuscular theory and the physiology of animal spirits. In leaving the *physical* causal story to the scientists, Locke nevertheless was greatly concerned with another causal story: the *psychological* causes of our thoughts and ideas. In general, he describes his method for constructing that story as an "Historical, plain Method", addressed to "the discerning Faculties of a Man, as they are employ'd about the Objects, which they have to do with" (1.1.2). The historical method, Locke hoped, would enable him to give an "Account of the Ways, whereby our Understandings come to attain those Notions of Things we have". He also sought to discover some "Measures of the Certainty of our Knowledge, or the Grounds of those Perswasions, which are to be found amongst Men, so various, different, and wholly contradictory".

What Locke labelled his 'historical, plain method' is an application to mental processes and psychological contents of the descriptive methodology of the Royal Society scientists. He sought to describe through careful observation and attention just how the mind works in receiving some ideas, in constructing others, in associating, comparing, abstracting, compounding still others. Locke employs this methodology in the service of what Hume later called 'the science of man'. Hume followed Locke in insisting that "this science . . . must be laid on experience and observation".[3]

Locke thought his enterprise might also be useful to other sciences in clarifying some of their terms and assumptions. He was modest in his statement of how his work was related to physical science, to such *"Master-Builders"* as Boyle, Thomas Sydenham (a medical doctor with whom Locke worked closely), Christian Huygens and Newton (*Essay*: Epistle to the Reader). Perhaps he could serve as an *"Under-Labourer in clearing the Ground a little, and removing some of the Rubbish, that lies in the way to Knowledge"*. Descriptive psychology (or descriptive cognitive psychology) might be a way of characterizing a large portion of the *Essay*, but Locke also gives much attention to an account of the use of words (with some recommendation for good word usage), as well as to developing an account of knowledge which is supportive of the methodology of the Royal Society.[4]

The *Essay* ends with a three-fold classification of disciplines, of what he refers to as 'sciences': the sciences of nature, action and signs. Signs include both words (linguistic signs) and ideas. The theory of signs includes an account of language (the way in which words function in relation to the ideas for which they stand; words as sounds and as signifiers; incorrect use of words; etc.) and a presentation of ideas (how they arise, different kinds, their relations to objects). A general rule of method throughout this work for directing the understanding to knowledge and clarity is: be sure that there are ideas for the words you use, and that those ideas are clear. Another general methodological rule which was especially important for the science of nature is: derive your ideas from the things themselves by means of patient and careful observation. Locke applies this rule to his account of the science of mind.

He identified and discussed three methodologies for the science of nature. The first method, the one he and the Royal Society rejected, was the method of appealing to books and authorities, rather than to observation and experience. Included in this method was the notion that logic could yield knowledge: the notion that knowledge is obtained by the use of rational principles (e.g. 'what is, is', 'the same thing cannot both be and not be') with the help of formal syllogisms. Locke was emphatic in his rejection of formal logic as a tool for science. There are in the *Essay* some suggestions for an informal logic which might play a positive role in knowledge and understanding.[5]

A second method for the science of nature was the appeal to metaphysical concepts rejected by Locke: substantial forms, real essences, two substances. Along with these concepts there went the notion of necessary connections in nature and the belief that, could we discover the real essences, we could have a deductive or demonstrative science of nature. Locke seems to have accepted this part of that methodology, although he did not think we were able to acquire such a demonstrative science. He did accept the notion that, were it possible, the knowledge of the internal constitution of bodies (*his* real essences), would yield a non-observational science of nature.

The third method Locke identifies is that of careful observation and the elaboration of what he called 'natural histories', a descriptive account of processes and events, of what qualities go together, of concomitances and correlations. This was the method to science Locke accepted, he applies it to the study of the human understanding. That method yields some particular certainties but no general, certain truths. General or universal certitude is contrasted with experimental certitude. That nature is uniform and acts in accordance with laws (laws set by God), is a truth Locke accepted, but not part of our knowledge.

> The Things that, as far as our Observation reaches, we constantly find to proceed regularly, we may conclude, do act by a Law set them; but yet by a Law, that we know not: whereby, though Causes work steadily, and Effects constantly flow from them, yet their *Connexions* and *Dependencies* being not discoverable in our *Ideas*, we can have but an experimental Knowledge of them. (*Essay*, 4.3.29)

It was, as we have seen, a general principle of Locke's metaphysics that all that exists is particular. That metaphysical doctrine was reinforced by his account of our knowledge of nature, which limits such knowledge to the objects and concomitances we are able to observe. Were a universal knowledge of nature possible because we had discovered real essences, it would seem that the particularist metaphysics might be upset: real essences might be the ontological counterpart of our abstract ideas and classifications. In the absence of such a knowledge of real essences, universality and generality belong only to ideas, to those ideas constituting systems of geometry or morality. Of the two kinds of knowledge obtainable by man – particular or general – particular knowledge can only be acquired through observation; general knowledge results from the conclusions we draw from the relations of our ideas. We are able to be certain of the truth of general propositions only when *"we know the precise bounds and extent of the Species its Terms stand for"* (4.6.4). Locke was, as we have seen, prepared to accept the corpuscular theory as the most probable on the nature of body and the causes of perception, but a knowledge of body in terms of corpuscles was not possible for man.

In order to have a knowledge of the real essence of body, it would be necessary to discover the size, figure and texture, as well as the motions of the active parts of body (4.6.12). Without a specific knowledge of the microscopical, insensible parts of our body, we are unable to affirm with certitude that *"all Men sleep by intervals*; That *no Man can be nourished by Wood or Stones*; That *all Men will be poisoned by Hemlock"* (4.6.15). We can draw probable conclusions of these sorts, but never certain, general truths. What Locke is claiming is that general truths are what Hume later called 'relations of ideas', not 'matters of fact'. General knowledge belongs to conceptual connections, to Locke's mixed modes. The definition of knowledge Locke gave placed the stress upon our perceiving the relations of ideas *"Knowledge* then seems to me to be nothing but *the perception of the connexion and agreement, or disagreement and repugnancy of any of our Ideas"* (4.1.2). The term 'perception' places the emphasis upon knowing rather than upon knowledge, upon the active aspect of acquiring knowledge, not the passive state of possessing it. There are two reasons for this emphasis: first he rejects the usefulness of formal logic and syllogistic demonstrations, and second, he insists that *"the Mind*, in all its Thoughts and Reasonings, hath no other immediate Object but its own *Ideas"* (4.1.1). The doctrine according to which ideas are the immediate object of the mind when it thinks, reasons, or is aware in any form, led some of his contemporaries (and has led some later philosophers as well) to question the possibility of scientific realism. The 'way of ideas' (as Locke's reliance upon ideas as a basic term in his theory of knowledge came to be called) seems blocked by an account of knowledge and perception rooted in the immediacy of ideas and their representative or sign function. Nevertheless, Locke was familiar with a Cartesian tradition (defended vigorously by Antoine Arnauld)[6] in which ideas were seen as representative of objects, in the sense of providing cognitive information about them, without rejecting direct realism. We shall examine this interpretation of ideas later.

Whatever we decide about the nature and role of ideas in Locke's definition of knowledge, it is important to recognize his interest in promoting a knowledge of nature, including human nature. At a time when many writers still tried to characterize knowledge in terms of formal logical principles, Locke substituted for that sort of logic a psychology of mental processes. He stressed the *natural* relations of ideas (in contrast with the *artificial* ones in logic) and the ordinary ways in which we think and associate ideas. The attack Locke made on the syllogism (on Aristotelian logic), argued that that logic is artificial, that it presupposes that we already know how to reason, that the logic rules do not aid discovery. These points had been made by Descartes and the authors of a popular modern logic, the Port Royal logic.[7] These writers defined logic as "the Art of well using Reason in the knowledge of Things", an art developed by reflecting on such operations of the mind as judging, reasoning, conceiving.[8] One finds the same rejection of the rules of logic here as in Locke. Just as we do not learn to walk by first learning a set of rules, so we do not reason by first learning the rules of syllogism.[9] In the same way, Locke added, children can best be taught a second language by simply speaking it and hearing it spoken, not by first learning the rules of its grammar.[10]

We learn to reason as we learn to speak. Locke did not believe thought necessarily depended on language, but he recognized the importance of a clear and precise language, as a means of communicating and expressing our thoughts. He places the stress upon our native ability to think and reason; there is no need for rules or valid argument forms. What *will* help is a presentation of propositions in such a way that their connection with other propositions can be easily seen. The *Essay* is not, as the Port Royal logic was, a treatise on the informal rules for the direction of the mind, but it does contain a few hints and some advice on how to think clearly. For example: (1) do not use words empty of meaning, without ideas; (2) simple ideas must be clear and distinct, complex ideas must be carefully formed before finding words to fit them (3) in so far as possible, use words in their ordinary, non-technical sense; (4) but recognize that there are times when it may be necessary to create new words, or to use old words in new ways; and (5) a fixed, standard meaning and use of words should be established.[11]

THE DEVELOPMENT OF AWARENESS

Locke's dismissal of formal logic as a tool for the sciences reflects a very fundamental change in the approach to knowledge and learning. Far from there being rules and principles on which our knowledge depends and from which it can be derived, Locke viewed the individual as a developing organism dependent upon the environment and upon the correct use of his faculties and talents. Many of his contemporaries maintained that some of the general rules and principles of reason and knowledge were innate, part of our native equipment. Other writers argued similarly for moral principles: they too were said to be innate. This popular innate doctrine claimed that the ideas of God, duty, and obligation are some of the first ideas a child has. In fact, if there are innate ideas or principles, they are the very first to enter the mind, having been acquired at zero time in the infant's development. Such untaught and unlearned ideas and principles ought, Locke argued, to be discernible among the early learned ideas and simple truths. The *Essay* can be seen as concerned with the conditions of knowledge and learning. In fighting the innate doctrine of his contemporaries (see Book One for his attack), Locke was not engaging in internecine battles with fellow philosophers; he was attacking a doctrine that challenged his whole conception of learning. That innate doctrine would make the teaching of religion and morals redundant. On the level of speculative maxims, such as the basic laws of thought cited by traditional logics, the innate doctrine would alter our notions of teaching and learning, since not only would children already understand such fundamental principles as 'it is impossible for the same thing to be and not to be', but they could derive further truths from these principles by deduction. Under pressure, the innatist usually retreated to saying that custom, tradition and environment were important for the child in that they helped to bring out the knowledge of those innate ideas and truths. Such a concession was of little effect against Locke, since he wished to show the consequences of that doctrine, especially for learning and teaching. The retreat, in any event, would not save the doctrine.[12]

In concluding his discussion of the innate doctrine, Locke tells us that he will next give attention to the foundations of knowledge and attempt to "raise an Edifice uniform, and consistent with it self" (1.4.25). He disclaims any "undeniable cogent demonstrations" in his alternative account, but points out that, if one were to accept his principles, he too might proceed in the usual way of demonstrations. He makes no pretence of demonstrating those principles, nor does he claim self-evidence for them. He does think that those principles are sound conjectures and that each of us can check them against our own experience.

It has never been very clear what are the principles to which Locke refers at the end of Book One, though the usual opinion is that he refers to the doctrines of simple and complex ideas, compositionalism, representationalism, and that all ideas come from experience. These interesting, troublesome (and, as they have become, 'canonical' for what goes by the name of 'empiricism' in most secondary literature) doctrines may be the principles on which the edifice of human understanding is based, but there is clearly discernible in Book Two a number of other principles, general ones about the time order of idea genesis, which are more probably the principles Locke meant to cite. There is no systematic presentation of these principles or of the time order for ideas, but one can extract a clear order from many passages.

As in his treatment of innatism, Locke's discussion of idea genesis centres around children and infants. There are several passages where Locke lays down his general views about the development of the minds of children. He was confident that "Whether we can determine it or no, it matters not, there is certainly a time, when Children begin to think" (1.2.25). Locke rejects that curious notion of some of his contemporaries, that the soul always thinks (2.19). He sketches the general pattern of development in this way:

> Follow a *Child* from its birth and observe the alterations that time makes, and you shall find, as the Mind by the Senses comes more and more to be furnished with *Ideas*, it comes to be more and more

awake; thinks more, the more it has matter to think on. After some time, it begins to know the Objects, which being most familiar with it, have made lasting Impressions. Thus it comes, by degrees, to know the Persons it daily converses with, and distinguish them from Strangers; which are Instances and Effects of its coming to retain and distinguish the *Ideas* the Senses convey to it. (2.1.22; cf. 1.4.13)

This account of the early development of the child's awareness speaks of observing as a way of discovering or tracing the acquisition of ideas in children. In 1.2.25, Locke seems to suggest (though, inside the polemic, it is difficult to determine if Locke speaks in his own voice) that the thoughts of children "are unknown to us", but in 1.2.27 he says unequivocally that it is certain the thoughts of children lie "open fairly to every one's view". In 1.4.2, he says if "we attentively consider newborn *Children*", we can perceive "How, by degrees, afterwards, *Ideas* come into their minds". Attentive considering as a method is again cited in 2.1.6 as a way of concluding what ideas a newborn infant has. In the same chapter, Locke also says that observation and experience disclose little evidence that the newborn child thinks very much; the conclusion in this case being helped out by the remark that infants sleep a lot. Later, from the observed fact that children always turn their eyes to the light "lay them how you please", Locke concludes that the idea of light is one of the first post-natal ideas (2.9.7).

The thought of children does frequently lie fairly open to us; observation of their behaviour and attentive reflection can yield a knowledge of the minds of our children. But these methods can hardly establish the time order of idea genesis in a specific child, and even greater difficulties stand in the way of generalizing a time order for all children. Moreover, that children have thoughts or ideas (to say nothing of truths, which Locke also claims they have), even in the earliest days and in the womb, could not be established by these methods. There is a certain amount of reasonableness in the order Locke suggests, but his account rests heavily upon specific principles. These principles are explicit in the *Essay* and constitute, I would suggest, the theoretical foundations of that edifice he promised to construct.

A general commonsense principle guiding Locke's analysis is that the ideas a child acquires come from objects in the child's environment, in particular those objects relevant to the needs and interests of the child (2.4.7). Pleasure and pain are, for Locke, general guides throughout life, operating even in the womb. They guide the acquisition of ideas as well as the formation of a virtuous character. Locke's second principle of idea genesis is that ideas come before the propositions of which they form parts (1.4.1). A third learning principle is that the more abstract and general ideas are acquired later than the less abstract and general ones; particular ideas and propositions are the first to be acquired (2.1.5,6). Within the second and third principles there are further divisions, but these three compose the framework for his views on idea genesis.

The time order begins in the womb, where Locke says he thinks the fetus may have "some faint *Ideas*, of Hunger, and Thirst, and Warmth, and some Pains" (1.4.2). He is more forceful in this claim at 2.9.5 when he says that he has no doubt that children in the womb received these ideas (see also 2.9.6,7; 2.10.5). But on the whole, "a *Foetus in the Mother's Womb, differs not much from the State of a Vegetable*", since "there is little or no variety or change of Objects, to move the Senses" (2.1.21). Light, as we have seen, is one of the very first post-natal ideas a child receives. Whether this idea comes before the particular ones of qualities (such as white, black, sweet, bitter) is not clear (1.4.3). The ideas of qualities do occur before the "Memory begins to keep a Register of Time and Order" (2.1.6). Other particular ideas occurring early, but after those of qualities, are those of the child's nurse, his cradle, and his toys (1.2.27).

Having ideas, though necessary, is never, for Locke, sufficient for knowledge. The early life of the child is marked by some knowledge, as well as by acquiring ideas. Locke's formal definition of knowledge as the perception of specific relations of and between ideas is applied to the earliest levels of awareness. To have the idea of 'sweet' is to be aware of that quality, to recognize it, and to re-identify it in our own experience. We can hardly do all this without also realizing that this idea differs from the idea of 'bitter', assuming we have also experienced bitterness. Just as soon as the child's mind is able to retain and receive distinct ideas, simple truths like "Sweet is not Bitter" are known (1.2.15,16). A child's knowledge of truth of this sort does not require the use of language: it is prelinguistic. Other similar truths that Locke seems to group with the prelinguistic ones are: "That a Rod and Cherry are not the same thing" (1.2.16), "that the *Nurse* that feeds it, is neither the *Cat* it plays with, nor the *Blackmoor* it is afraid of" (1.2.25), that "the *Wormseed* or *Mustard* it refuses is not the Apple or Sugar it cries for" (1.2.25), "that Wormwood rubb'd on the Nipple hath not the same Taste, that it used to receive" (1.4.3), and that "Mother is not a stranger". If some of these truths require the ideas of identity or 'the same', as two of them do in the form in which Locke gives them, then they cannot occur at this stage in the child's development. What is important to note is that Locke believes children do acquire knowledge, even before they learn language. By saying that a child *knows* these truths (whose constituent ideas are particular), Locke means to say more than that the child responds in certain ways. Recognition is not thought of as dispositional or behavioural; it is a mental state. This prelinguistic mental state exemplifies the first kind of knowledge relation cited by Locke, that of identity or diversity. Having any of the simple quality ideas involves seeing that the quality is what it is and is different from other such qualities. The formulation of this sort of knowledge can, of course, only be done in propositions, but the knowing is non-linguistic. The mental state of knowing is thus propositional, involving a 'that' form: "that Sweet is not Bitter".

Locke introduces these claims for early knowledge in the context of his discussion of innatism, a knowledge that is really the correlative of having any idea. The innatist had claimed, in effect, that children know (at least have the ability to know early) abstract speculative principles about same, different, equal, and also moral principles about duty and obligation. Knowing that equals added to equals are equal is quite different from knowing that sweet is not bitter. Sweet is a direct sense impression, but equal is an abstract general idea, not the direct content of sensation. Having the idea of equality or of identity also differs from having sensory ideas. According to Locke's theory of the time order of idea genesis, memory, comparison, and the use of language are necessary before we can know the truths of the propositions cited by the innatist.

Locke does recognize that religious and moral principles are installed into the unprejudiced understanding "either by the open

Profession, or tacit Consent of all" that the child has to do with (1.3.22). That is precisely the role of education. Such moral teaching even begins before memory "began to keep a Register of their Actions, or date the time, when any new thing appeared to them" (1.3.23) Locke does not say the child *knows* such family principles. He presumably refers here to behaviour, though it would be quite in keeping with his learning theory to say that the child knows that such and such is bad. 'Know' would more closely approximate the 'know' in the sweet-bitter example, though 'bad' tends to be an abstract idea and hence to occur later. Custom and habit within the family are what Locke has in mind in discussing the early teaching of religion and manners.

Before a child can know the abstract and general principles cited by the innatists, he must acquire the abstract, general ideas and names that are ingredients in those principles. The order is: abstract ideas before general principles (1.2.12), general names after abstract ideas (1.2.15). 'Man' and 'animal' are general ideas (3.3.7), 'equality', 'impossibility', and 'identity' are general names (1.2.16). Each name has a corresponding idea; but Locke specifies that one acquires ideas before names, just as some knowing is prelinguistic. There are important exceptions to the principle that ideas are acquired before names. In the "beginning of Languages, it was necessary to have the *Idea*, before one gave it the Name" (3.5.15), but now, being born into a society that has a language, children frequently acquire names before they find the ideas with which they are associated. The precedence of names over ideas is, Locke says, found especially in the more difficult and complex ideas of actions and character traits. "What one of a thousand ever frames the abstract *Idea* of *Glory* or *Ambition*, before he has heard the Names of them," (*ibid.*). For most moral words, "the sounds are usually learned first"; the meanings (that is, the ideas) are attached by adults relating them to the sounds, or else the child learns what they mean by his own observation and industry (3.9.9). There is a constant danger in learning the name before the idea – the danger of speaking "words no otherwise than Parrots do" – but careful attention in teaching can avoid this pitfall (3.2.7). One main function of education is to help children to acquire virtue and good manners. One facet of that learning is attaching names to those actions that parents and tutors praise and blame.

Language learning and naming are important for Locke's general account of the human understanding. Knowing and speaking are closely linked. The order appropriate for learning moral words is insufficient and ineffective for learning to name the things and qualities the child confronts in his environment. In order to make knowledge more precise and accurate, we must be sure our ideas fit the nature of things. Our language for expressing that knowledge must then conform to the use in our society. Getting our ideas right requires careful attention to experience and observation.

> A Child having taken notice of nothing in the Metal he hears called Gold, but the bright shining yellow colour, he applies the Word Gold only to his own *Idea* of that Colour, and nothing else; and therefore calls the same Colour in a Peacocks Tail, Gold. Another that hath better observed, adds to shining yellow, great Weight: And then the Sound Gold, when he uses it, stands for a complex *Idea* of a shining Yellow and very weighty Substance. Another adds to those Qualities, Fusibility: and then the Word Gold to him signifies a Body, bright, yellow, fusible, and very heavy. (3.2.3)

Such close fitting of ideas to things follows the way we ordinarily teach children the meaning of thing and quality words: "People ordinarily shew them the thing, whereof they would have them have the *Idea*; and then repeat to them the name that stands for it, as *White, Sweet, Milk, Sugar, Cat, Dog*" (3.9.9). The acquisition of ideas of things comes about easily since "Children, when they come first into it, are surrounded with a world of new things, which, by a constant solicitation of their senses, draw the mind constantly to them" (2.1.8). Parents should aid their children's learning process by acquainting them with the variety of objects in the environment. Sensory deprivation will severely limit the number and kind of ideas a child acquires. For example,

> if a Child were kept in a place, where he never saw any other but Black and White, till he were a Man, he would have no more *Ideas* of Scarlet or Green, than he that from his Childhood never tasted an Oyster, or a Pine-Apple, has of those particular Relishes. (2.1.6)

Similarly, "I doubt not, but if a Colony of young Children should be placed in an Island, where no Fire was, they would certainly neither have any Notion of such a thing, nor Name for it" (1.4.11).

Locke also speculates that the same colony of children would not come across other persons on their island with an idea of God and would not acquire such a concept themselves "til some one amongst them had imployed his Thoughts to enquire into the Constitution and Causes of things" (1.4.11). Such an enquiry can come only late in the order of acquisition of ideas; the idea of God is too abstract and complex to appear early in the genesis of ideas. All ideas are particular, but some can be made to stand for others, thereby gaining generality. The operation of applying the ideas of nurse and mother to other persons requires the child to notice that "there are a great many other Things in the World, that in some common agreements of Shape, and several other Qualities, resemble their Father and Mother" and their nurse (3.3.7). Once these general and abstract ideas and names have been acquired, propositions follow, less general ones (e.g. *"That One and Two are equal to Three*; *That Green is not Red"*:1.2.19) before more general ones (e.g. *"it is impossible for the same thing to be, and not to be"* 1.2.20). Even among these more general propostions there is a time order, speculative before practical. The reason for this last order is interesting: "Those speculative Maxims carry their own Evidence with them: But moral Principles require Reasoning and Discourse, and some Exercise of the Mind, to discover the certainty of their Truth" (1.3.1).

THE ACTIVE MIND

We noted earlier in this chapter the distinction Locke drew between ideas or appearances and their referents and causes. In those passages where he cites or uses a physical or physiological explanation, he always contrasts those physical processes with the mental acts and contents of the mind. When he says, for example, that the senses convey *"into the mind*, several distinct *Perceptions* of things"*, he explains that 'convey' means that the senses carry into the mind "what produces there those *Perceptions"* (2.1.3). Presumably what he means is that the stimulus gets to the mind, or attracts its attention, by means of the sensory equipment of the body. He ends 2.1.25 by speaking of the sensory impressions having ideas annexed to them, but he remarks that it is the ideas that are perceived, although the mind is said to *receive* the impressions.

His use of the phrase 'the mind' and the talk of impressions being conveyed to the mind should not be read in a substantive way, as if it designates a thing or substance. In many passages, 'the mind' is simply meant to refer to that aspect of the individual which is aware, conscious in some particular way. Where we are more inclined to say 'Jones was not aware of that noise', or 'Smith was reflecting on his sensations', Locke, and most writers in the seventeenth and eighteenth centuries, tended to speak of the mind or the understanding performing these functions. These writers also spoke of particular 'faculties' of the mind, such as reason, memory, or imagination, tracing specific types of mental activities to specific faculties. For the most part, we can translate such talk of faculties of the mind, and the talk of the mind itself, into talk of mental acts performed by people. In the example just cited, it is clearly some particular perceiver who becomes aware of some sensory input and who *attends* to that input.

The question of how one attends to the physical reports of the senses, if in fact that is what Locke meant to say, remains unanswered. He may only have meant to indicate that some acts of awareness are triggered by physical and physiological events. To settle for correlations between physical and mental events would, I suspect, have been considered too weak by Locke; but whether he would insist on hanging on to a *causal* connection, or whether he saw himself as part of a developing tradition which began to replace causal relations with significatory or semantic relations, is difficult to determine on the basis of his texts. What we can say is that in his account of awareness, mental processes play a most active and decisive role in the genesis of ideas. Even in the case of simple ideas of sense, the mind must be attentive to what the senses report, or else that report will go unrecorded or will be recorded only at the neural level (2.1.6,8; 2.9.3). In 2.1.23 Locke tends to underplay the role of attention, by defining sensation as "an Impression or Motion, made in some part of the Body" (that is, as a physiological or brain event) which "produces some Perception in the Understanding" (that is, which produces some awareness). He says that the mind employs itself about these impressions; but if these impressions are physiological, it could employ itself only about the perceptions produced by those impressions. The transition from nerve impulse to conscious content occurs, but Locke does not have much to say about how it is accomplished. One point is clear: the awareness of ideas is acomplished through the cooperative interaction of objects, neurophysiological processes, and awareness.

'Perception' is Locke's term for awareness. It is the first act of the mind exercised about its ideas. It is also a term sometimes used to refer to a faculty. An 'idea' may be viewed as a conscious mental content. Despite Locke's remark in 2.10.2 that ideas are nothing "but actual perceptions in the mind", he has not confused the faculty with that which is produced by that faculty. Act and content, faculty and object of the faculty are distinguished. Without the act there can be no content, and conversely, without a content there can be no act. There are no contentless acts. Being conscious and having ideas are simultaneous conditions. Quite apart from the question of whether we are aware of objects in the environment or only ideas in our minds, Locke saw the importance, for a theory of thinking, of stressing the first elementary act of recognition. To be aware is to be aware of some content of the mind, the simplest form of such awareness is what he describes as perceiving "each *Idea* to agree with it self, and to be what it is; and all distinct *Ideas* to disagree, *i.e.*, the one not to be the other" (4.1.4).

There are many other operations of the mind besides simple awareness, operations that play their role in the generation of more complex ideas. But we must not understress the part played by simple awareness; appreciation of its importance will help overcome the mistake of saying that the mind for Locke is wholly passive. He *did say* that it is wholly passive, but he could not have meant it in the sense in which it has been taken, that is, that the stimulus is inscribed upon the mind, or results in an awareness *of* some content, without any help at all from the mind, without the perceiver being active in any way. In 2.1.4 Locke speaks of the operations of the mind (such as perception, thinking, doubting, believing, and many others) as actions. In 2.1.10 he reformulates the question, 'is the mind always thinking?', as 'is the mind always in action?'. The mind is "fitted to receive the Impressions made on it", but no impressions will occur unless we attend to the stimulus (2.1.24). The image of the "white Paper void of all Characters" (2.1.2) is and has been misleading, if taken to mean that the mind starts from scratch. The white paper image was an alternative to innatism which considered the mind filled with ideas and truths at birth. Locke went out of his way in Book One of the *Essay* to say he was not denying "natural tendencies imprinted on the Minds of Men", tendencies to seek happiness and avoid misery (1.3.3). The *Education*, as we have seen, makes much of many natural personality traits that characterize different children. The *Conduct of the Understanding*, as does the *Essay*, speaks of natural faculties: "We are born with faculties and powers capable of almost anything." The mental faculties to which Locke appeals are the most important supplement to the white paper metaphor: it is by the action of the faculties that characters become inscribed on the mind, that we become aware of ideas.

   Much misunderstanding has plagued generations of readers of Locke about the image of the white paper and the passivity of the *tabula rasa*. They were unfortunate images. A careful look at the text clarifies what Locke meant by the *tabula rasa* image. Physical objects surrounding us "diversely affect" our sense organs and "the mind is forced to receive the Impressions" (2.1.25). But though this intrusion of impressions into the mind is not something we can prevent by willing, neither is it independent of other mental operations. In fact, it is "the Operations of our minds" that "will not let us be without, at least some obscure Notions" of those impressions. Passivity, then, means involuntariness: it also means that we cannot invent new impressions or destroy acquired ones without some physical help (see 2.2.2; 2.12.1; 2.22.2; 3.5.2). I cannot conjure up a taste "which had never affected" my palate "or frame the *Idea* of a Scent" that I have never smelled (2.2.2). When that taste or smell does reach my awareness, the mind is not inactive, but being active is not synonymous with exerting active power. Thus, when I see the moon or a star, or feel the heat of the sun, I am not acting on the moon or star or sun and bringing about changes in them, as I am when I move a book, raise my hand, turn my eyes away from the moon, or remove my body from the sun. In these latter instances, "I am properly active; because of my own choice, by a power within my self, I put my self into that Motion" (2.21.72).

The passivity of the mind does not rule out its activity, although its action in perception is not of the same nature as intentional action. Nevertheless, the mind or the perceiver is not passive in the way that a wax tablet might be said to be passive. The action of attending to sensory reports also may differ from the attending involved in self-awareness, in becoming aware of one's thought processes. In reflecting on our thought processes, in acquiring ideas of thinking, perceiving, believing and reasoning, there are no obvious sensory impressions to attend to or to leave impressions on the mind. But in both sensation and reflection, we become aware of ideas, not sensory or neural impressions.

What Locke wanted to say was that external sensible objects and internal operations of the mind are the things and processes upon which the attentive faculty of the mind is directed and from which ideas are derived. We have yet to consider whether his use of ideas as apparent media between the perceiver and objects will make it possible for him to say we are aware of and can observe objects. But his general programme for the derivation of ideas says that knowledge is both *founded in* and *derived from* two sources, sensation and reflection. He characterizes these sources of ideas and knowledge as two 'fountains' (2.1.2). The ideas that are derived from these two sources are derived with the help of the mind as well as under the stimulus of objects. Those ideas fall roughly into two groups: simple and complex. The programme for the derivation of complex ideas reveals that there is a rather marked difference in the way ideas arise from experience (where 'experience' includes both the fountains) when they are complex and when they are simple. But both require acts of the mind.

Simple ideas arise in, or – a most revealing and important phrase – are 'suggested to' but not made by, the mind. To understand Locke's programme for the derviation of ideas (to see whether he has shown how all ideas come from experience, as he claims), and to appreciate the role of mental operations in that derivation, we need to take some specific examples of the derivation of ideas and analyse them carefully. The examples I shall take are quite different from those Locke used in his discussion of the development of awareness in infants and children. It is not clear from the text where in the time order Locke would place the ideas in these examples. He does not relate them to children or to the developmental psychology implicit in much of what he writes, but these ideas do throw

considerable light on the way the mind works and its role in
knowledge.

Solidity

We derive the idea of solidity from the sensations of touch and
resistance. Locke calls attention to the fact that in all our postures
we are aware of a support to our body. Solidity becomes the
"*Idea* most intimately connected with, and essential to Body"
(2.4.1). The idea of pure space arises in conjunction with body
and solidity as follows: a man conceives of two bodies at a
distance such that they could move towards one another and
touch edges. This thought gives us the idea of space without
solidity by a kind of intellectual operation or experiment. If we
then think of one body moving without its place being
immediately filled, we have the idea of pure space. Sensation and
reflection have been used in the genesis of these two ideas, and
sensation and reflection are what Locke means by experience.

Space and Number

The derivation of an idea such as pure space by reflection differs
from the derivation of other ideas by that means. We reflect upon
our own mental operations and in that way obtain the ideas of
thinking, willing, or doubting. We employ the mental operation
of reflection in order to obtain these reflective ideas. But we also
employ reflection and many other mental faculties in obtaining
many ideas of sense. Pure space is one such example, the ideas of
existence and unity are two more. Locke says that these two latter
ideas are *suggested to* the mind "by every Object without, and
every *Idea* within" (2.7.7). The idea of 'one' is another example
of an idea not derived directly and immediately from sense.
Locke says "every *Idea* in our Understandings; every Thought of
our Minds brings this *Idea* along with it" (2.16.1). This, then, is a
tandem idea, one idea joined to others. No distinct
neurophysiological process stands behind the idea of 'one'. The
acquisition of any idea by sensation brings another along with it.
Another tandem idea is that of 'finite': "The obvious portions of
Extension, that affect our Senses, carry with them in to the Mind
the *Idea of* Finite" (2.17.2). The idea of substance as something

over and above the sensible qualities is the most notorious tandem idea in Locke's account: he speaks of the mind being forced to think of a subject as a unifying entity for the qualities. Whether Locke as a philosopher accepts the idea of substance, he has, he thinks, described how our mind does reach such an idea.

Existence and Power

Suggestion is surely not the straightforward derivation from sensation or reflection that Locke seems to have in mind when he first states his programme. If we take some external object and say that it 'suggests' existence and unity to the understanding, it would seem that Locke could not mean to say that there is some physiological process whereby this idea is generated. What is involved is a kind of tandem or joint process: along with some of our sensory ideas come further ideas when we are suitably attentive and advanced in thought. We 'consider things as there', which is how he describes the idea of existence, but this 'considering' is a rather sophisticated mental operation. Locke makes frequent appeals to these mental operations or acts of 'considering', 'taking notice', 'reflecting', 'concluding'. The idea of power is a paradigm case of the genesis of an idea with the help of these sorts of mental operations.

> The Mind, being every day informed, by the Senses, of the alteration of those simple *Ideas*, it observes in things without; and taking notice how one comes to an end, and ceases to be, and another begins to exist, which was not before; reflecting also on what passes within it self and observing a constant change of its *Ideas*, sometimes by the impression of outward Objects on the Senses, and sometimes by the Determination of its own choice; and concluding from what it has so constantly observed to have been, that the like Changes will for the future be made, in the same things, by like Agents, and by the like ways, considers in one thing the possibility of having any of its simple *Ideas* changed, and in another the possibility of making that change; and so comes by the *Idea* which we call *Power*. (2.21.1)

These acts of the mind (considering, concluding, etc.) do not tie the mind to sensation or to any straightforward act of reflecting or introspecting: they work independently of the two fountains of experience, generating a host of ideas. When Locke comes to the derivation of our ideas of mixed modes (e.g. moral concepts), he clearly is dealing with a derivation in which the mind is even more independent of sensation and reflection. They are (or at least can be) framed by the mind without reference to what really exists, either outside or within the mind. The transition to such a generation or creation of new ideas is an extension of those appeals to considering, concluding, comparing in the derivation of the idea of power. The freedom from experience which Hume later gave to the imagination is assigned by Locke to 'the understanding' in general. "The Understanding, in the consideration of any thing, is not confined to that precise Object: It can carry any *Idea*, as it were, beyond it self, or, at least, look beyond it, to see how it stands in conformity to any other" (2.25.1). Just what is involved in 'carrying' ideas or in 'looking beyond' them is not made clear. He proceeds to show how our ideas of causal relations are derived from but go beyond sensation. We observe in sensation that some things bring other things into being; for example, heat is the cause of the fluidity of the wax. A cause is "that which makes any other thing, either simple *Idea*, Substance, or Mode, begin to be" (2.26.2). Thus, Locke has shown how the relational idea of cause and effect arises from sensory experience together with an act of the mind. "For to have the *Idea* of *Cause* and *Effect*, it suffices to consider any simple *Idea*, or Substance, as beginning to exist " (*ibid*). It is this 'considering' that assists the process of acquiring these ideas. The idea that arises in this case, as in the examples of substance and power, could be said to be an explanatory idea: it makes sense of the experiences we have.

The active mind was consistent with Locke's general belief in a purposive universe. God would not give us faculties of mind if he did not intend us to use them. The innate doctrine was irresponsible since it would leave man with faculties which are able to discover truth but which are made redundant, at least with respect to those important speculative and moral truths of which the innatists were so fond. There is a parallel for Locke between the agency of the person in accepting responsibility for moral actions and the actions of the mind in assuming responsibility for knowledge and the acquisition of ideas.

NOTES

1 In *Descartes' Philosophical Letters*, trans. and ed. Anthony Kenny (1970), p. 138.
2 See also his *Rules for the Direction of the Mind*, rules VIII, XII.
3 *A Treatise of Human Nature*, ed. L.A. Selby-Bigge (2nd edn revised by Peter Nidditch, 1978), Introduction, p. xvi.
4 For an extended study of this latter aspect of the *Essay*, see my *Locke and the Compass of Human Understanding* (1970).
5 For a discussion of Locke's suggestion, see *ibid.*, pp. 92–102.
6 See Arnauld's *Des vrayes et des fausses idées* (1683).
7 La logique ou l'art de penser (1662). The citations are from the English translation of 1685, p. 41. See also Descartes' *Rules*, VIII, IX, X, XII.
8 *Ibid.*, p. 41.
9 *Ibid.*, p. 80.
10 *Education*, §168.
11 Book 3 of the *Essay on Human Understanding* is devoted to these and other comments about language and thought.
12 For an account of the innate doctrine and Locke's attack on it, see my *John Locke and the Way of Ideas* (1956).

7

Ideas and Knowledge

When we piece together the various accounts of the acquisition of ideas, we discover four main types of ideas discussed by Locke. Each type plays a specific role in his account, always with some acts of the mind involved. (1) Some of the ideas relate to children, to the learning process, to the early stages of the development of awareness. The acquisition of early ideas also yields some truths and some knowledge which the child acquires through the ideas in his awareness. (2) Other ideas relate to self-knowledge, to learning about our own mental operations, enlarging our knowledge of the human understanding. Both these types of ideas help fill out the science of mind. (3) A third class of ideas found in Locke's derivation programme plays an explanatory role, helping to make sense of experience, linking one experience to others (e.g. the ideas of cause, substance, power). (4) Still other ideas relate to scientific observation, to the science of nature, expressing Locke's endorsement of the methodology of the Royal Society, reaching knowledge of the world through experience and observation.

EXPERIENCE AND THE REALITY OF KNOWLEDGE

When Locke asks, early in Book One of the *Essay concerning Human Understanding*, "Whence comes it [the mind] by that vast store [of ideas], which the busy and boundless Fancy of Man has painted on it, with an almost endless variety?" (which was the same as asking "Whence has it all the materials of Reason and Knowledge?"), he replied emphatically: "To this I answer, in one word, From *Experience*" (2.1.2). The term 'experience' covered both sensation and reflection, so his answer to these questions claims that "we have nothing in our Minds, which did not come in, one of these two ways" (2.1.5). After a discussion of complex ideas (the ideas of substances, relations, mixed modes), he concluded confidently:

> If we will trace the progress of our Minds, and with attention observe how it repeats, adds together, and unites its simple *Ideas* received from Sensation or Reflection, it will lead us farther than at first, perhaps, we should have imagined. And, I believe, we shall find, if we warily observe the Originals of our Notions, that even *the most abstruse* Ideas, how remote soever they may seem from Sense, or from any operation of our own Minds, are yet only such, as the Understanding frames to it self, by repeating and joining together *Ideas*, that it had either from Objects of Sense, or from its own operations about them: So that those even large *and abstract* Ideas *are derived from Sensation, or Reflection*, being no other than what the Mind, by the ordinary use of its own Faculties, employed about *Ideas*, received from Objects of Sense, or from Operations it observes in it self about them, may, and does attain unto. (2.12.8)

What we have seen from the few examples selected for study is that Locke's programme of deriving all ideas from experience is fundamentally dependent upon what he calls in this passage "the ordinary use" of the mind's own faculties. He even goes on to show how ideas that seem "the most remote from" the ordinary ideas of sense and reflection, e.g. the ideas of space, time and infinity, can be accounted for in the same way. In many cases, the derivation is experienced-based only in the sense that, when confronted with certain phenomena or appearances, the mind runs through specific operations with the result that it constructs a new idea. It is especially important for those readers who are tempted to apply to Locke the label of 'empiricist' to recognize the complex and involved acts of mind required before ideas in group 3 above are formed. In a narrow but rather traditional interpretation of the term 'empiricism', these ideas seem to go beyond what that label is used to mean. Group 3 ideas go beyond experience in that they ascribe a cause, a power, or a substance to events, an ascription not warranted by what can be observed in those events. I observe objects behaving in certain ways and then, after reflecting and appealing to a principle of causation, conclude that there are causes or powers at work. I experience certain groups of qualities uniformly and repeatedly occurring together and conclude (or feel constrained to conclude) that there is a subject to which they belong.

It was that sort of move beyond what is experienced that Hume later attacked. Our ascriptions of substance over and above qualities, of a self over and above a string of perceptions and mental acts, of objects over and above appearances: these Hume traced to the active faculty of imagination which bridges gaps in our experiences, adds features (or covers over their absence) to what is available to us by experience and observation. Hume's imagination (which he characterizes as a 'magical faculty') creates fictions that help make sense of our experiences. Hume does not reject all those fictions, since he does clearly believe in a self, external objects, and real causes, but the fact that it is the faculty of imagination which helps explain or make sense of appearances is an interesting change from the seventeenth-century account of the role of that faculty.

There are for Locke some rather strict limitations on the imagination, although it does serve some purposes. For example, we are unable to "fancy any Taste" which has never affected our palate (2.2.2), but a musician is able to "put together silenty in his own Fancy" strings of separate notes to form a tune (2.18.3). Mixed mode ideas, the ideas for actions, can be acquired by seeing two men wrestle or fence, but we can also invent them, as "he that first invented Printing, or Etching, had an *Idea* of it in his Mind, before it ever existed" (2.22.9). We can also acquire mixed mode ideas by having someone explain to us "*the names* of Actions we never saw, or Notions we cannot see; and by enumerating, and thereby, as it were, setting before our Imaginations all those *Ideas* which go to the making them up" (*ibid.*). As we have seen earlier, classes are our devising; the species of actions in particular are the "Creatures of the Understanding, rather than the Works of Nature" (3.5.12). Thus, "When we speak of *Justice*, or *Gratitude*, we frame to our selves no Imagination of any thing existing" (*ibid.*). This contrast between the creatures of the imagination and the works of nature is important for Locke. We must be attentive to which domain our ideas refer. Unlike the "abstract *Ideas* of those Vertues", when "we speak of a *Horse*, or *Iron*", we should not think of those ideas as referring only to the mind, they refer to "Things themselves".

When it comes to knowledge, especially knowledge of nature, the imagination is useless and can interfere. Knowledge is sharply contrasted with 'fancying', guessing or believing (4.1.2). In addressing the topic of the reality of our knowledge of nature, Locke raises what seems to be another criterion question: how can I be sure that my ideas are not just the imaginations of my brain, an extravagant fancy (4.4.1). He even reflects his censure of religious enthusiasts by adding to these descriptions of our putative ideas of reality, "the Visions of an Enthusiast". Locke recognizes that a man can talk coherently and consistently but not move beyond "the agreement of his own Imaginations". The seeming criterion question turns out to be a phenomenological or descriptive one: are there experiences which convince us of the reality of their objects? Remarking on the fact that some sensory ideas are forced upon us, as when I look on the sun by day or feel the warmth of the fire at night, he claims that such experiences give us certain knowledge that these ideas have been caused by something other than ourselves: they are not "the Actions of [our] Mind", or mere fancies (4.11.5). The ideas we acquire under those sorts of conditions are not, he assures us, "*Ideas* floating in our Minds, and appearances entertaining our Fancies" (4.11.6). The experience of being burnt yields a similar conclusion.

> He that sees a *Fire*, may, if he doubt whether it be any thing more than a bare Fancy, feel it too; and be convinced, by putting his Hand in it. Which certainly could never be put into such exquisite pain, by a bare *Idea* or Phantom, unless that the pain be a fancy too. (4.11.7)

Men generally, but scientists in particular, "would not be thought to talk *barely* of their own Imaginations, but of Things as really they are" (3.2.5). A knowledge of nature will and must be found in things themselves, "not in our Imaginations" (3.11.24). Similarly for truth: it must be more than the joining of words to make grammatical sentences, which may conform well enough to "*Chimaeras* of Men's Brain" (4.5.7). Truth is affirming propositions which conform to things. *Real* truth is distinguished from chimerical truth, *real* knowledge from "the visionary World in our own Imaginations" (*ibid.*). Part of Locke's way of distinguishing real from chimerical knowledge is by identifying different faculties. The faculty of imagination yields 'fancies' and 'fictions', the faculty of sensation is closely linked with reality. Simple ideas of sense (those in group 1 above) are not, we learn through experience, able to be made by us: they force themselves upon our attention and "must necessarily be the product of Things operating on the Mind in a natural way" (4.4.4). The sensory appearances correspond to or 'answer' "that Power which is in any Body to produce" that particular appearance. He does not say that the ideas of whiteness and bitterness tell us that some object is white and bitter, only that there is an object which has the causal power to produce those ideas in perceivers.

The uniformity of appearances, the regularity of conjunctions of qualities in our experience, is all we need to construct a descriptive science of nature. Since Locke has dispensed with real or natural classes, he only needs to urge us to be good observers of phenomena. The careful recording of coexistent qualities, the systematic agreement on conventions of classification, the sharing of our recordings with other observers: these are the ways in which the only real knowledge of nature possible for us can be achieved. In the science of nature, we cannot arbitrarily put properties together and call something 'gold'. We must copy nature. Since knowledge of real essences (even of Locke's corpuscular nature) is impossible for man, our ideas of objects must be "taken from the Works of Nature" (4.4.11). Good observers, exact and detailed observations, are not always easy to find, but what the works of nature are for Locke are the very things themselves as observed and experienced by us, ideas or appearances.

It is this merging of ideas with appearances which has worried many readers of Locke, especially philosophers. With his acceptance of the corpuscular theory and the doctrine of qualities as powers, Locke is committed to a *specific*, not just a *numerical*, difference between physical reality (matter and physical objects) and the appearances of that reality, between powers and experienced qualities. Can he in fact draw this distinction between the qualities of objects and the ideas of those qualities? The more basic question is: have the appearances of material reality been turned into ideas? There are passages in the *Essay* where it sounds as if the answer to the first question is no, and the answer to the second is yes. At the very end of that work, after defining a sign as that which "the Mind makes use of for the understanding of Things", he goes on to say:

> For since the Things, the Mind contemplates, are none of them, besides it self, present to the Understanding, 'tis necessary that something else, as a Sign or Representative of the thing it considers, should be present to it: and these are *Ideas*. (4.21.4)

When he defined knowledge, it was said to be the *perception* of the relation of *ideas*. In the chapter on 'the reality of our knowledge', Locke asked whether his account of our knowledge of nature has not resulted only in "a Castle in the Air" (4.4.1). He puts the question to himself, "Knowledge, say you, is only the perception of the agreement or disagreement of our own *Ideas*: but who knows what those *Ideas* may be?" (*ibid.*) Those ideas may be just fictions of the imagination. The question then seems to be, "How shall the Mind, when it perceives nothing but its own *Ideas*, know that they agree with Things themselves?" (4.4.3). His answer to this last question is the one we have just traced: simple ideas of sense indicate through their independence from our will that they are caused by something in nature. Those ideas are signs or appearances, appearances which enable us to "distinguish the sorts of particular Substances, to discern the states they are in, and so to take them for our Necessities, and apply them to our Uses" (4.4.4).

It is clear from all that Locke says in these passages that, while the works of nature are not themselves present to the understanding, their appearances *are* present. Those appearances are signs of what does not appear. Sensory qualities are appearances and signs of powers in matter. A power is unlike its manifestation. The *power* to cause perceivers, who have neurophysiological equipment of a specific sort, to see red is not itself red. The same remark applies to perceptions of sounds, tastes and smells. The account seems to be different for qualities such as figure, extension, texture, bulk, motion: these were called by Locke "primary or original qualities". The *ideas* of these qualities are said to be "*Resemblances*" of the qualities, "and their Patterns do really exist in the Bodies themselves" (2.8.15). Locke says explicitly that "we perceive *these original Qualities*" in those bodies large enough to be sensed (2.8.12). Yet, 'perceive' is distanced from the qualities by the causal process of motion in nerves and brain. It is the *motion* in the nerves which is carried to the brain and which produces in our minds the particular ideas of figure, extension, etc. Motion, then, seems to be responsible for the specific ideas of those original and primary qualities. It is insensible particles which come from objects to sense organs and 'convey' the motion to nerves and brain.

The causation of the ideas of colours, sounds, and tastes is also corpuscular motion. Those tiny, insensible bodies are figured and extended, they have a specific bulk and they move, but it seems from Locke's account that it is the *motion*, not the figure, bulk, or extension which causes the ideas of both kinds of qualities, the primary and these latter which are called 'secondary'. However, in his account of the causation of the ideas of secondary qualities, he speaks of the "different Motions and Figures, Bulk, and Number" of the insensible particles "affecting the several Organs of our Senses". This passage sounds as if the figure, bulk, and number of the particles play a causal role, along with their motion. The example he gives suggests that reading:

> that a Violet, by the impulse of such insensible particles of matter of peculiar figures, and bulks, and in different degrees and modifications of their Motions, causes the *Ideas* of the blue Colour, and sweet Scent of that Flower to be produced in our Minds. (2.8.13; cf. 2.8.16,17)

But he ends this example by reference to motion only:

> It being no more impossible, to conceive, that God should annex such *Ideas* to such Motions, with which they have no similitude; than that he should annex the *Idea* of Pain to the motion of a piece of Steel dividing our Flesh, with which that *Idea* hath no resemblance.

The annexation talk refers at least to the correlations between motion and ideas; it may not rule out causal connections between the properties of the particles striking the sense organs and the ideas in the mind. Nevertheless, the annexation is said to be to the *motions*, not to the peculiar figure, bulk and number.

A further puzzle emerges when we notice that this same causation is said to be the source for the ideas of primary as of secondary qualities. Does God play an annexing role also in the case of the ideas of the figure, extension, or motion of some object? Is it *different* particles, or particles of different *degrees* of figure, bulk, extension and motion which account for my idea of blue, from those that account for my idea of the figure of the violet? Locke did not develop the details of the theory of the physical causation of ideas, beyond this rough account. Motion is the most likely candidate for the stimulus in nerves and brain, for there is no indication in what Locke writes, or in any of the other writings employing this theory, that the shaped and figured particles get inside the sense organs. Still, it may be that that theory supposed that the figure, extension and bulk of the particles gave some special quality to the motion of their impact on the sense organs, such that the different degrees of figure and bulk, along with the different motions, accounted for different ideas at the terminus of this causal process.[1] Some writers avoided the details of the theory by denying any causal connection between physical and mental: God's annexing or conjoining ideas with certain kinds of sensory processes was taken as mere correlation. For these writers (Malebranche is one), the only causation was God's. But Locke does seem to want to retain a causal connection between objects and ideas.

It is that causal connection which, when experienced as ideas forced upon our attention, convinces him that sensory ideas are real. What it means to say they are real is just that something else besides ourselves is responsible (at least in part) for their origin. This much is true of both kinds of ideas, those of primary and those of secondary qualities. When Locke says that the former ideas *resemble* their qualities, while the others do not, he appears to be adding another claim to the belief in external causes, the claim that when ideas of primary qualities are present to the understanding, we can say not only that the object has the power to produce those ideas in my awareness, but also that I know the figure, extension, texture, and motion of some real object. Never mind that this knowing may seem mediated by a causal process, whereby the figure, bulk, extension and motion of the particles of the desk somehow enable me to acquire an idea of those qualities of the desk, not of the particles. In saying that the desk *appears* rectangular and three feet long, I am saying as well that it *is* that shape and that size. In saying it *appears* brown, I am *not* saying it *is* brown, only that it has a power to appear brown.

The works of nature, the physical objects that surround and act upon us, do have, in themselves and apart from perceivers, the primary and original qualities. Those works also have the two kinds of powers, those that act on perceivers and those that act on objects. The most general statement about the objects that comprise our world is that they have qualities and powers. This general statement is not of much use to science, except in so far as someone like Boyle sought to use the corpuscular theory as an explanation of the appearances and behaviour of the objects of science. But the more productive aspect of the science practised by Locke's friends and acquaintances was the descriptive part, the careful and detailed account of what qualities regularly appear together, what happens when gold or lead is tested in various ways. The theory behind the observed changes was considered to be of less importance than getting correct the natural histories of colour or gold.

There were opticians who sought for an account of the workings of the eye in visual perception. Few of these paid attention to the actual experience of seeing. Berkeley, early in the eighteenth century, criticized the standard optical theories for this oversight. Prior to Locke, Descartes developed an account of light and the perception of light which appealed both to neurophysiological theory and to the experience of seeing objects: he combined physiology with psychology. Locke follows this same new approach, trying not to be drawn into too much physical detail because he wants to focus on the psychology of perception. That psychology, the account of sensing as well as those natural histories of the acquisition of ideas, Locke saw as consistent with the method to science followed by the Royal Society. It was consistent in being descriptive, but it was also consistent in its focusing on the way in which the works of nature appear to us.

WHAT ARE LOCKE'S IDEAS?

That worry which has plagued many philosophers about whether we perceive the works of nature as they are in themselves was not a concern for Locke. His quick answer to the sceptic who questions whether all our experiences may be dream and illusion (they "may dream that I make [them] this answer", as he traced his account of simple ideas of sense; 4.11.8) has been viewed by these philosophers as an irresponsible dismissal and a begging of the question. There should be, these philosophers say, *arguments* proving the existence of an external world. Locke should have seen, they continue, that he can hardly accept the talk of insensible particles and a causal theory of perception, if he is going to insist that all our knowledge arises from sensation and reflection. Furthermore and here is their trump card – Locke's ideas block direct access to the physical world, they are a screen or veil between the perceiver and the world.

This interpretation of Locke has been associated with the representative theory of perception, the theory that speaks, as Locke does, of ideas representing objects. The representation stands in for what it represents, that of which it is a sign. At best, the talk of ideas as a screen or veil is a metaphor, at worst it is very misleading. We speak of an eclipse of the sun or moon, where one planet blocks the view of the other. We are familiar with obstructions to our view of some object or event. These are *visual* blockings. One sound can block out another. The Berlin wall blocks, or slows access to, a city. We might also want to consider the limitations of our eyes and ears – the limited range of light and sound waves they can respond to – as another sort of barrier, one that instruments circumvent. On Locke's corpuscular account of matter, we have sensory access to secondary qualities but not to the causal powers which help produce them. Not even the primary qualities reveal the corpuscular structure of their causes. So, on Locke's own account, reality does differ from its appearance. This difference, however, is one we are all familiar with. If that is all the charge of Lockean ideas being a screen or veil amounts to, there would be nothing any more worrisome about that account than about any recent scientific theory.

But, it will be remarked, in my short list of barriers to perception, I have not cited Locke's ideas. Are these not a different sort of barrier from the examples above? There are many problems with the account Locke gives of knowledge by means of and through ideas, but one feature of his ideas usually overlooked is their identification with appearances. We saw earlier Locke writing 'ideas or appearances'. The term 'idea' includes, but is not exhausted by, the sensible appearances of objects. One of the questions is, do ideas differ from qualities? With secondary qualities (colour, sound, taste), the *quality* part is the power in objects to cause those appearances, those sensory ideas in perceivers. With primary qualities (extension, bulk, texture), while the causation of our perception of them is the same as for the perception of secondary qualities (corpuscular), the object we see *is* extended in the way in which my idea of that extension indicates. The appearance to me of that object is a correct or true appearance. It is still an appearance. I am being appeared to (to use one locution in vogue) in a primary- and a secondary-quality way. Both appearances have a physical and a psychological causal origin. The result of these two causal processes is a sensory appearance characterized by colour, shape, size, bulk, etc. By paying close attention to all aspects of that complex appearance we can construct an account of the uniformities and correlations of those appearances. Those appearances *are* the world of descriptive science, they are the bases for our classification of objects into kinds.

Where is the *representation* in ideas taken as appearances? Ideas for Locke are signs, so how do we make the sign-signified distinction when ideas become appearances? We might point to Locke's remark about the reality of simple ideas: that they are real because they are caused by something other than ourselves. The feature of these ideas which shows their causal origin outside me than seems to be a sign feature. I do not believe this is the feature of ideas Locke meant to identify as their sign quality. Locke was a close reader of Descartes and of some controversies among Descartes' followers, especially the controversy over the nature of ideas betwen Antoine Arnauld and Nicolas Malebranche.[2] Malebranche turned Descartes' ideas into rather odd sorts of objects existing in the mind of God. When we have the experience of perceiving a physical object, God sees to it that the appropriate idea is placed in our awareness, along with the sensory impressions caused by that object. The theory of Malebranche is obscure, but both Arnauld and Locke took him to be distorting Descartes' ideas; they both interpreted Malebranche's ideas as proxy objects preventing direct access to physical objects. Both Arnauld and Locke strongly disavowed this sense of 'idea', insisting that what that term meant in their writings was simply the perception, the awareness, of physical objects or their qualities.

Arnauld distinguished between a *spatial* presence of objects and a *cognitive* presence. Physical objects obviously cannot be spatially present to the mind, but they can be cognitively present. It is their cognitive presence which is captured by ideas. Ideas are mental contents, significatory, sign-bearing, in the sense of being cognitively meaningful. The causal relation between the works of nature and our neurophysiological equipment is joined in conscious perception by this cognitive relation.[3] To say that we know objects by means of ideas is to say no more than that objects become known through sensory awareness. If the indirectness sometimes charged to Lockean ideas is simply this fact that objects are mediated by awareness, then sceptics can find no support in that fact. Recognizing this fact about our cognitive access to objects does not, of course, overlook the need to sort true from false perceptions, but the route to follow for checking on the accuracy of our perceptions is the route Locke stressed: careful, repeated observations, which is the method to science recommended and followed by Locke. Knowledge of the works of nature by means of ideas can be real and true if we are good observers.

CONCLUSION

Locke applied this descriptive scientific methodology to awareness. He was attempting to write the natural history of the human understanding, taking the full range of its faculties and operations, from the earliest vague sensations in infants to detailed accounts of the origin of complex and abstract ideas, from the beginnings of self-consciousness to a full science of mind. Just as those scientists who turned their attention to physical phenomena (whether chemical, geological, medical or astronomical) sought for precise desciptions, so when Locke turned his hand to human consciousness (feelings, beliefs, knowledge), he initiated the beginnings of cognitive psychology.

The same curiousity which led Locke from some brief reflections on knowledge in 1671 to the elaborate *Essay concern-*

ing Human Understanding can be seen at work wherever he turned his attention. Whether he was examining the Bible for what it says about doctrines required of a Christian, reading St Paul's Epistles for an understanding of what Paul said in Paul's own terms, seeking the best ways to guide a young child to virtue and knowledge, addressing the issues of civil and religious authority, tracing the conceptual move from communal to private property, or even elaborating that important distinction between man and person: in these and most of the areas he investigated, Locke succeeded in cutting through old prejudices and in casting new light on fundamental human questions. He was not entirely free of assumptions, of beliefs that were not always supported by his descriptive methodology: the belief in necessary connections in nature, in the Great Chain of Being, in the interconnection of all things in nature, that reason is natural revelation. He held some basic hopes about man: that we can become responsible moral agents, that our faculty of reason can control our passions, that reason can work with God's laws of nature to build a stable political society.

Locke's personal life was exciting, politically active and, I would guess, satisfying to him. The systematic investigation into the diverse areas of his studies must have been equally satisfying. Having said this, it would be wrong to conclude that there are no internal problems in any of his books, that the issues he confronted were solved in ways that will meet our needs or demands for intellectual rigour. But we can say that he was not timid in his approach to those issues, nor in rejecting old orthodoxies when they seemed unwarranted, nor in venturing new ideas when they promised to be useful. Two important themes stand out from his writings: the theme of the appropriating consciousness of the person in becoming morally responsible for his own actions, and the theme of the need to understand others in their own terms. Whether Locke himself fulfilled either of these themes (I think he did well by the first, not so well with the second), a careful study of his thought is worth our attention.

NOTES

1 See Descartes' *Rules for the Direction of the Mind,* rule XII, where

figure, not motion, is the explanation of differences in our perception of the qualities of objects.

2 See Malebranche's *De la recherche de la vérité* (1678) and Arnauld's *Des vrayes et des fausses idées* (1683).

3 For an elaboration of this interpretation of seventeenth- and eighteenth-century accounts of perception, see my *Perceptual Acquaintance from Descartes to Reid* (1984).

Bibliography

LOCKE'S MAJOR WORKS

(listed in order of publication)

A Letter concerning Toleration, trans. William Popple from the Latin original (London, 1689).

Two Treatises of Government: In the Former, The False Principles and Foundation of Sir Robert Filmer, and his Followers, Are Detected and Overthrown. The Latter is an Essay concerning the True Original, Extent, and End of Civil-Government (London, 1690). The edition used in this study is *A Critical Edition with an Introduction and Apparatus Criticus*, by Peter Laslett (Cambridge, 1960).

An Essay concerning Human Understanding. In Four Books (London, 1690). The edition used here is the Clarendon Edition edited by Peter H. Nidditch (1975).

Some Considerations of the Consequences of the Lowering of Interest and Raising the Value of Money (London, 1692).

Some Thoughts concerning Education (London, 1693). Citations are from the edition of James L. Axtell, *The Educational Writings of John Locke* (Cambridge, 1968).

The Reasonableness of Christianity, as Delivered in the Scriptures (London, 1695).

A Letter to Edward Lord Bishop of Worcester, concerning Some Passages Relating to Mr. Locke's Essay . . . in a Late Discourse of His Lordship's in Vindication of the Trinity (London, 1697).

Mr. Locke's Reply to the Right Reverend the Bishop of Worcester's Answer to His Letter (London, 1697).

Mr. Locke's Reply to the Right Reverend the Bishop of Worcester's Answer to His Second Letter (London, 1699).

A Paraphrase and Notes on the Epistles of St. Paul . . . To Which is Prefix'd, An Essay for the Understanding of St. Paul's Epistles, by Consulting St. Paul Himself (London, 1705–7).

Posthumous Works of Mr. John Locke (London, 1706). Contains, among other items, "An Examination of P. Malebranche's Opinion of Seeing All Things in God", and "A Discourse on Miracles".

The Works of John Locke (London, 1714, 3 vols.). The 1823 edition (10 vols.) has been used in this study.
An Early Draft of Locke's Essay, edited by R.I. Aaron and Jocelyn Gibb (Oxford, 1936). P.H. Nidditch has more recently edited this draft, *Draft A of Locke's Essay concerning Human Understanding*, transcribed with Critical Apparatus (Department of Philosophy, University of Sheffield, 1980).
Essays on the Law of Nature, The Latin Text with a Translation, Introduction and Notes, edited by W. von Leyden (Oxford, 1954).
Two Tracts on Government, edited with an Introduction, Notes, and Translation by Philip Abrams (Cambridge, 1967).
The Correspondence of John Locke, edited by E.S. De Beer. In Eight Volumes. Clarendon Edition of the Works of John Locke (Oxford, 1976-. Volume 8 has not yet appeared).

FURTHER READING

There is an extensive literature of writings on Locke, ranging from his own time to the present. Two recent bibliographies can be consulted: Roland Hall and Roger Woolhouse, *80 Years of Locke Scholarship* (1983) and Jean S. and John W. Yolton, *John Locke: A Reference Guide* (1985). A few specialized books of recent vintage are listed below.

Colman, John, *John Locke's Moral Philosophy* (Edinburgh, 1983).
Dunn, John, *The Political Thought of John Locke: An Historical Account of the 'Two Treatises of Government'* (Cambridge, 1969).
Franklin, Julian H., *John Locke and the Theory of Sovereignty. Mixed Monarchy and the Right of Resistance in the Political Thought of the English Revolution* (Cambridge, 1978).
Tully, James, *A Discourse on Property. John Locke and his Adversaries* (Cambridge, 1980).
Vaughn, Karen Iversen, *John Locke, Economist and Social Scientist* (Chicago, 1980).
Yolton, John, W., *John Locke and the Way of Ideas* (Oxford, 1956).
—— *Locke and the Compass of Human Understanding* (Cambridge, 1970).
—— *Perceptual Acquaintance from Descartes to Reid* (Oxford and Minnesota, 1984).
—— *Thinking Matter: Materialism in Eighteenth Century Britain* (Oxford and Minnesota, 1984).

Index

I am grateful to James G. Buickerood for his assistance in compiling this index.

Aaron, Richard I., 73
Abbot of St Martin, 110
Abrams, Philip, 14, 91
actions, 53, 55, 64, 88, 98, 103, 129, 142; appropriated by persons, 68–70, 74; indifferent, 76; intentional, 135; of men, 59–60, 63, 83; of objects, 108; two concepts of, 114; virtuous, 39, 51, 72, 138; words for, 53–6
Acworth, Richard, 15
Adam, 35, 59, 69, 80
agent, 70, 97, 98, 114, 115
angels, 87, 99, 106
animal(s), 17, 24, 32, 35, 59, 61, 64, 72, 88, 109, 112
animal spirits, 111, 117, 119; *see also* physiology
anthropology, 70
appearance(s), 117–19, 131, 141, 142, 144, 145, 149–50
archetypes, 40, 41, 42, 44, 43–56, 108; *see also* standards, mixed mode(s)
Arnauld, Antoine, 15, 122, 150–1, 153; controversy with Malebranche, 3
assent, 88
atheism, 79, 91; Locke accused of, 4
Axtell, James L., 32

Bagshaw, Edward, 2
belief(s), 14, 18–19, 30, 152; and knowledge, 94–9, 117, 121, 147; religious, 45, 75, 78–9, 81–4, 88, 97, 99

Berkeley, George, 148
Bexwells (Stringer's house), 11
Bible, 36, 77, 92–4, 97; as containing doctrines necessary for a Christian, 78–82, 103, 152; and revelation, 87–91, 96; as source of moral rules, 34–5, 43, 50, 75
Boyle, Robert, 5, 101, 111, 120, 148
brain, 19, 24, 26, 88, 99, 108, 132, 143, 146–7
Burnet, Thomas, 5, 15; his *Remarks*, 3
Burthogge, Richard, 4

Cain, 61
Cambridge Platonists, 46
Cartesians, *see* Descartes, René and Cartesianism
Castor, 26
cause(s): of ideas, 118–19, 122, 131, 146–7, 150; as powers, 111–15, 117, 141–2; of qualities, 102, 108
certainty, 94, 97
chain of being, 109-10, 152
changelings, 105, 107, 108; *see also* monsters
children: and the acquisition of truths, 123, 125–31, 135, 140; and desires, 22–4; and moral education, 52–3, 57, 58, 71, 82, 124, 152; their natural traits and tempers, 19–21; should read the Bible, 35; and reason, 39, 47, 58, 64, 72, 124; rights of, 36–7, 69
Christ, Jesus, 43, 50, 78, 80, 81, 82,

85, 87, 90, 91; his Sermon on the
    Mount, 81–2
Christ Church, Oxford, 6, 13, 45
Christianity, 34, 43, 50, 79, 80, 81–2,
    91, 92, 93, 96, 97, 103, 116, 152
church; of Christ, 78, 81; and the
    magistrate, 76; the nature of
    the, 77, 93; as a society, 59, 78
Cicero, M. Tullius, 50
Clarke, Edward, 5–8 *passim*, 11, 12,
    13, 15, 58
Clarke, Mrs Edward, 13
classification, 104–5, 107, 118, 121,
    144
community, 59–60, 63, 64–6, 70; of
    mankind, 63, 67, 72, 79
concept(s) 55, 56; of actions, 53–6;
    metaphysical, x
consciousness: as a basis for personal
    identity, 28–32, 38, 56, 70, 72,
    96, 152; distinguished from
    memory, 32; and the mind, 19
consent, 66, 70, 75, 129
contract: marriage, 58; social, 66, 75
corpuscular hypothesis or theory,
    99–100, 104, 110-11, 119, 122,
    144
Cranston, Maurice, 6, 15
criticism: Locke's reaction to, 3, 4–5
Cudworth, Damaris (Lady
    Masham), 8–10, 99
Cudworth, Ralph, 9, 99
Culverwel, Nathaniel, 46
custom(s), 51, 52, 55, 58, 76, 77, 129

De Beer, E. S., 15
demonstration, 40–2, 49, 53, 83, 86,
    88, 90, 121, 122, 125;
    distinguished from deduction,
    40; in Euclid, 42, 86; and
    knowledge, 83, 88, 125; of
    morality, 41, 49, 53, 90; and the
    science of nature, 121
Descartes, René and Cartesianism,
    18, 25, 40, 118, 122, 123, 139,
    148, 150, 152
desire(s), 19, 21, 22, 24, 39
duty (duties), 72; of parents, 35; of
    the state, 57; *see also* rights

education, ix, 5, 14, 19, 20, 23–4, 25,

43, 52–3, 58, 64, 71–2, 129;
    moral, ix, 34–9, 55–6, 57
Egyptian sorcerer, 85
Elizabeth, Princess, 118
empiricism, 125, 141
enthusiasm, 45, 88, 89, 143; versus
    reason in faith, 9
essence, 96, 100, 103–5; moral,
    104–5, 108; real, 94–5, 104, 106,
    120, 121, 122, 144
Euclid, 40, 42, 43, 85, 86
Evelegh, Anne, 8
evidence, 83, 86–7, 89, 93, 98
experience: and belief, 83–4; and
    knowledge, 25, 110–11, 116,
    119–20, 125–7, 130, 140–2; and
    the origin of ideas, 135–8;
    reflective, 18; sense, 47, 48; and
    truth 43–4, 45–6, 108
experimentation, 5, 101

faculties; inborn, 48; of men, 24, 64,
    83, 106, 119, 124; of the mind,
    34–5, 45, 132–5, 138, 141–2,
    144, 151; natural, 20, 47, 85–7,
    134;
faith, 9, 45, 76, 77, 78–82, 82–7, 94,
    97; defined, 85; *see also* religion
Filmer, Sir Robert, 2, 6, 35, 36, 50,
    59, 68–9
France, 4, 11, 13
freedom, liberty, 53, 62, 67, 74, 75,
    76, 115; and government, 42;
    and law, 36–7, 59–60; in the
    state of nature, 63–4, 68–9; of
    wives, 58

Gibb, Jocelyn, 73
God, 21, 42, 56, 59, 69, 72, 74, 80,
    82, 83, 93, 105–6, 115, 117, 138,
    146–7, 150; idea of, 22, 48, 131;
    and innate principles, 19, 35, 36;
    knowledge of, 2, 49; his law, 29,
    44–6, 50, 60, 81, 121, 152; mind
    of, 150; and miracles, 84–7; and
    scale of being, 109; and thinking
    matter, 98–100, 112–13, 116;
    word of, 34, 79, 90, 94; worship
    of, 76–7
government, 57, 59, 63, 64, 68, 74,
    91

gravity, 112
Greenhill, John, 11–13
Griggs, Mrs, 7

habit(s), 55–6, 72, 129
happiness, 21–2, 28, 31, 35; concern
    for, 26, 29
Hercules, 26
Hobbes, Thomas, 57, 59, 99;
    Hobbist, Locke charged as, 4
Holland, 4, 6, 7, 8, 10, 11, 13, 15
Hooker, Richard, 37, 60
human nature, 21, 22, 24–5, 35, 44,
    51, 58, 61, 62, 72, 110, 123
Hume, David, 119, 122, 138, 142
Huygens, Christiaan, 5, 119
hypotheses, 44, 104, 112

ideas(s), 1, 18–19, 27, 32, 92–3, 95,
    97, 135, 138; abstract, 95–6,
    104, 121, 127, 128, 129, 131; of
    actions, 53–4, 115; cause of,
    119, 131; clear and distinct, 94;
    complex, 54, 103, 105–6, 107,
    113, 125, 133, 141; in
    demonstration, 40; general,
    128, 129; genesis of, 46, 53, 125,
    127–32, 137; of God, 124;
    innate, 50; moral, 41–5, 56;
    nature of, 3; qualities, 100, 102,
    103; reflective, 136; relations of,
    86, 103, 122; their role in
    knowledge, x, 117, 123, 140–52;
    sensory, 128, 143; simple, 85,
    111–13, 125, 132; way of, 122
identity, 17, 25, 28, 94, 128, 129;
    personal, 25, 28–32, 38, 94–6
imagination, 18, 132, 138, 142–4, 145
immaterial substance, 94, 98–9, 100,
    101
immortality, 98, 99
individualism, 67, 72
innate; knowledge, 124, 125, 128;
    principles, 129, 138; truths, 46,
    47, 48, 50, 108, 134
intention(s), 19, 30, 54–5, 56
intuition, 83; intuitive knowledge, 86

John, St, 80
judgement, 56, 57, 83
justice, 41, 42, 60

Kelly, Patrick, 14
Kenny, Anthony, 139
knowledge, 55, 76, 82–4, 93, 94, 97,
    98, 103, 107, 109, 122, 124, 126;
    children's 37; and experience, 5,
    121, 135; God as the source of,
    45; of good, 23–4; of happiness,
    26; and ideas, x, 3, 117–19, 123,
    127, 138, 140–52; innate, 46;
    intuitive, 86; of the law of
    nature, 48, 64; moral, 41, 51;
    and revelation, 86, 89; theory
    of, 89, 92, 120, 123; of truth, 79

labour, 68, 70, 71, 72, 73
language, 53–6, 72, 92–3, 95–6, 110;
    scientific, 55
Laslett, Peter, 2, 7, 14
law(s), 36–7, 42, 54–5, 124; civil, 38,
    48–9, 51–2, 58, 59, 60, 66, 67,
    70, 72, 75, 76, 78; of faith, 80,
    81; of fashion, 52; of God, 28,
    29, 39, 41, 45, 46, 51–2, 76, 121;
    moral, 2, 28, 48–9, 51–2, 75; of
    nature, 2, 35, 37, 38, 46, 47,
    48–9, 50, 57, 59–64, 65, 67, 69,
    71, 72, 75, 81, 84; of opinion or
    reputation, 51–2; of reason, 35,
    38, 45, 61, 63, 64, 75, 81–7; of
    right, 81; of works, 81
LeClerc, Jean, 4
life, 24, 66; same, 17, 97
Locke, John; epitaph, 2, 5, 14,
    15–16; his investments, 14;
    moral censor, Christ Church, 2,
    45; personality, 2, 8; as
    Philander, 8–10; portrait, 10–
    13; professes his love of truth, 5
logic, 104, 119–24; Aristotelian, 123;
    Port-Royal, 123
Long, Thomas, 99, 116
Luke (New Testament), 81–2

machine, 17; of the body
    (mechanism), 18, 19
magistrate, 68, 75, 76, 91
majority, 66, 67, 75
Malebranche, Nicolas, 3, 15, 18,
    147, 150, 153; controversy with
    Arnauld, 3
man, 17, 24–8, 30, 34, 105–6, 107;

distinguished from person, ix, 38, 56,
98, 103, 152; moral, 23–4, 25,
27, 29, 34, 35, 52–3, 56, 57,
67–70, 74; natural, 65; same, 27,
28; science of, 119
mankind, 38, 45, 52, 60, 63, 64–5
Masham, Damaris, *see* Cudworth,
Damaris (Lady Masham)
Masham, Sir Francis, 10
materialism, 17, 99–100, 116
matter: as active, 116, 117, 144, 145;
corpuscular, 100, 104, 110, 114;
inorganic, 108; insensible, 84;
organized, 24, 99; parcel of,
105; particles of, 17, 97, 111; as
passive and inert, 115; and
thought, 98–100, 108, 113
Matthew (New Testament), 81–2
meaning, 95; ordinary meaning of
texts, 88
medicine, 6, 14
memory, 18, 26, 27, 38–9, 105, 127,
128, 129, 132
mental acts or operations, 18,
112–13, 114–15, 135, 136, 137,
140, 141, 142, 143
Messiah, 80, 81, 82
metaphysics, 18, 92–116
Middlesex County, Grand Jury of, 4
mind, 1, 23, 24, 39, 40, 53, 54, 89,
103; its distinction from the
soul, 18; faculties of, *see*
faculties; presence to, 151; its
relation to the body, 9; and
religious belief, 77, 82; science
of, 117–39
miracles, 80, 82, 84–5
mixed modes, 53–6, 72, 108, 122,
138, 141, 142, *see also*
archetypes, ideas
Molyneux, William, 4
monarchy, 69, 74–5; absolute, 63, 75
money, 2–3, 14, 36, 62, 70–1
monsters, 105, 110, *see also* changelings
moral: agent, 98; beliefs, 14, 75;
discourse, 55–6; life, 59;
relations, 51; rules and
standards, 34–50, 55–6, 75;
truths, 39–45, 46, 48, 90, 138;
truths, demonstration of, 39–40,
90

morality, 103, 131; Christian, 41;
Scriptural, 81
More, Henry, 46
mortality, 31
Moses, 84, 85, 86, 90
motives, 23, 24, 52, 55, 56
muscles, 18, 19, 24

names and naming, 53, 54, 95–6,
104, 129–31, 142; of substances,
103
natural kinds or classes, 109–10, 111
nature, 60, 70, 94–6, 105–8, 112, 114,
121, 145; human, 22, 24, 25, 35,
44, 51, 58, 61, 62; law of, *see* law
of nature; light of, 49; science
of, 120, 140, 144; state of, 56,
57, 59–61, 63–7, 72, 74;
understanding or knowledge of,
55, 143
nerves, 18, 19, 24, 108
Nestor, 29
Newton, Isaac, 5, 40, 112, 116, 120
Nidditch, Peter, 15, 73, 139
Noah, 86
Norris, John, 3, 5, 15

Oates (or Otes), 10
obligation, 56–7, 60, 75, 124, 128; of
the state, 57
observation, 5, 43–4, 101, 108, 119,
120, 121, 126, 129, 130, 140–4
optics, 4
Oxford, University of, 2, 4

pain, 21, 23, 24, 26, 28, 51, 127
parricide, 54
particulars, 105–11, 115, 121
passions, 9, 19, 21–4, 34, 39, 63
Paul, St, 1, 14, 79, 85, 87–8, 97, 116,
152
person, 14, 27, 39, 58, 62, 65, 71, 72,
97, 101, 102, 103; as agent of
actions, 55–6, 114–15, 138; and
consciousness, 38; corporate
and public, 57, 67, 68, 69, 72,
76, 77; distinct from man and
moral man, ix, 25, 34, 74, 98,
152; their immortality, 99; as
moral agent, 28–32, 41, 52, 55,
59, 82, 98; and nature, 94–6;

private, 67, 76, 78; as property, 68–9; two persons in one body, 26; viewing children as, 53, 57

physiology, 18, 21, 27, 108, 111, 114, 119, 131, 132–3, 137, 145, 148, 151

Plato, 26

pleasure, 21, 23, 24, 26, 28, 51, 53, 126

politics and political theory, 6, 56–7

Pollux, 26

Popple, William, 91

Portugal, Royal Censor Board of, 4

power(s), 74, 115, 117; absolute, 62, 69; active and passive, 112–13, 115–16; arbitrary, 68, 75; causal, 111–15; of the community, 64–6, 68; executive, in the state of nature, 60–3, 65–7; God's or divine, 85, 100; idea of, 103, 137–8, 141–2; of language, 55; of man, 106, 134; of matter, 112–13, 145; natural, 65, 68, 113, 117; of objects, 108, 115, 144, 147–8, 150; political, 59, 67, 76

preservations: of mankind, 62–3, 64; self-, 36, 62, 64; of young, 35

probability, 83, 87, 109

proof, 88

property (properties); ideas of, 102; of objects or substances, 53, 99–100, 101, 105; private, 67–72, 73, 152; and its protection, 42–3, 59

psychology, 54, 70–1, 118, 135, 148, 150, 151; affective, 27; cognitive, x, 18, 24, 120

punishment(s), 51, 52, 60, 61, 62, 71

quality (qualities) 105, 130, 151; and classes, 95, 106, 142, 144; ideas of, see *ideas*; primary and secondary, 113–14, 145–51; sensible, 100–1, 106–7, 108, 112, 117, 127, 128, 137; substances, 104, 113, 142

rationality, 20, 25, 27, 34, 35, 37, 39, 52, 74–91, 99, 107

realism; direct, 123; scientific, 122

reason, 37, 38, 60, 62, 76, 88, 91, 93, 97, 123, 140; age of, 36–7, 58, 64, 72; in animals and brutes, 109–10; as a faculty of mind, 45, 105, 132; and faith, 82–7; light of, 49, 89; and morality, 39–45; natural, 20, 89; as natural revelation, 45–50, 152; rule of, 61; versus desires, 22–4; as the voice of God, 35; see also law of reason

reflection, 94, 101, 126, 135, 136, 137, 138, 141, 149

Reid, Thomas, 153

religion, ix, 4, 14, 21, 48; 63–4, 74–91, 93–4, 99, 103, 124, 129; natural, 80; orthodox beliefs of, 4, 102; see also faith

responsibility, 56, 70, 96; of society, 57

Resurrection, 51, 94, 97–8

revelation, 45, 81, 84, 85-6, 88, 89, 90, 91, 92, 93–4, 96, 152; criterion for, 87–91, 92, 93–4; natural, 45–50, 89; original, 85, 86–7, 90, 91; traditional, 85, 87, 91

revolution, 67, 68

rights, 59, 60, 61, 62, 64, 65, 66, 70, 72; of children, 35; natural, 36–7, 75; and natural inclinations, 36; property, 70

Rousseau, J.-J., 57

Royal Society, 119, 120, 140, 148

St John's College, Cambridge, 15

scepticism, 4, 30

science, 6, 53, 101, 103, 105, 124, 148, 150, 151; demonstrative, 121; and hypotheses, 104; language of, 55; of mind, 117–39, 140, 151; of nature, 120, 144; scientists, 53, 119

Scriptures, 78, 79, 81, 82, 85, 87, 89, 90, 91, 92, 93, 94

Selby-Bigge, L.A., 139

self, 28, 29, 30, 31, 70, 142; see also person

Seneca, 9

sensation(s), 18, 94, 117, 118, 128, 132, 135, 136, 137, 138, 141, 144, 149, 151

Sergeant, John, 3, 5, 15
Shaftesbury, Anthony Ashley
  Cooper, Earl of, 6, 10, 11
Sherlock, William, 116
Sidney, Algernon, 6
sign(s), 85, 90, 149–51; ideas as, 92,
  120, 122, 145, 149–51; for
  miracles, 85, 90
Smith, Robert, 116
society, 51, 52, 53–6, 56–8, 63, 64,
  76; civil, 57, 58, 59, 60, 62, 65,
  66, 67, 68, 70, 74, 75; political,
  56–7, 59, 66, 72, 76–7; religious,
  75, 78
Socinianism, 4
Socrates, 26
soul: distinct from mind, 18;
  immaterial substance, 30, 94,
  98–9, 101–3; its relation to the
  body, 97; its relation to person,
  29; its role in the genesis of
  ideas, 46; salvation of, 75; as
  that which thinks, 24–8, 29, 118
space, 136, 141
Spinoza, Benedict, 99, 100
spirits, 99, 115
standards, 55, 64, 69–70, 76, 90; *see
  also* archetypes
state of war, 61, 62, 68
Stillingfleet, Edward, Bishop of
  Worcester, ix-x, 3, 4, 92–7, 99,
  100, 102, 103, 116
Stringer, Susan, 11, 13
Stringer, Thomas, 11–13
substance, 27, 31, 95, 100–3, 104,
  106, 107, 111, 114, 120, 138,
  142, 145; essence, 25, 94; idea
  of, 102, 112–13, 137, 141;
  immaterial, 18, 30, 98–9, 101
  and the Trinity, 96
substratum, 102, 103
Sydenham, Thomas, 5, 120

Thanet House, 11
theology, 9, 92, 93–8
Thersites, 29
thinking matter, 100, 116
Thomas, Dr David, 7

thought, 18–19, 24–8, 98–100, 108,
  113, 114
Toland, John, 96, 97
toleration, 73–7 *passim*, 79, 99
traits, character, 20, 24, 34, 39
Trinitarians, 96
Trinity, 94, 96–7, 116
tritheism, 116
Troy, 29
truth(s), 45, 48, 64, 79, 83, 88, 89,
  121, 122, 126, 131, 143;
  conceptual, 43, 86; innate, 46,
  124; known by children, 126–8,
  140; logical, 86; mathematical,
  40, 41, 85; moral, 41, 43–4, 46,
  90; and passion, 22; reached by
  natural faculties, 20, 86;
  revealed, 85–7, 89–91, 94, 96;
  self-evident, 46–7, 89; systemic,
  43–4; of the world, 40, 43
Tully, James, 73
Tunbridge Wells, 9
tutor, 23, 24–5, 52, 71–2
Tyrrell, James, 6

understanding, 25, 39, 52, 56, 83, 86,
  121, 125, 128, 130, 140, 151; and
  classes, 142; and demonstration,
  40, 42; differences in between
  men, 20; as a faculty, 18, 79, 89,
  105, 119, 137, 138; and ideas,
  117, 136, 145, 147; and the
  mind, 132; rational, 34
uneasiness, 21–2, 23–4, 35
Unitarians, 96

value, 70, 71
virtue: Christian, 81–2; and desire,
  21–3; and education, 25, 27,
  37–9, 52–3, 56, 72, 129; and
  rationality, 34–5, 44, 52; and
  religion, 77–82; Scriptural, 82;
  and socialization, 51
Von Leyden, Wolfgang, 14, 50, 91

will or volition, 59, 63, 69, 79, 101,
  115, 118; child's, 52; God's, 51;
  of the people, 57, 66
Willis, Thomas, 18